Peace of Mindfulness: Everyday Rituals to Conquer Anxiety and Claim Unlimited Inner Peace

Barrie Davenport

Disclaimer

Your Free Gift

As a way of saying thanks for your purchase, I hope you'll enjoy three audio guided meditations to further your practice of mindfulness in daily life. You'll read more about using guided imagery and meditation throughout this book. These audio meditations will help you with relieving anxiety, overcoming limiting beliefs, and nurturing self-esteem.

You can access the guided meditations by going to this site: http://barriedavenport.com/mindful-gift

Contents

About Barrie Davenport

Barrie Davenport is a certified personal coach, thought
leader, author, and creator of several online courses on
self-confidence, life passion, and habit creation. She is the
founder of two top-ranked personal development sites,
Live Bold and Bloom and BarrieDavenport.com. Her work
as a coach, blogger, and author is focused on offering
people practical strategies for living happier, more
successful, and more mindful lives. She utilizes time-
tested, evidence based, action-oriented principles and
methods to create real and measurable results for self-
improvement. You can learn more about Barrie on her
Amazon author page at barriedavenport.com/author.

Introduction

*"You must live in the present, launch yourself on every wave,
find your eternity in each moment.
Fools stand on their island of opportunities and
look toward another land.
There is no other land; there is no other life but this."*

~ Henry David Thoreau

I know you've just started reading this book, but stop for a moment and mentally review your day. Think about some of the specific activities you engaged in—brushing your teeth, making coffee, driving to work, talking with a coworker, going for a run. What were you thinking about during these activities? Can you remember anything that occupied your mind during the day? If you remember any of your thoughts, how many were focused on the past or the future, or were related to some negative incident or anxiety you replayed in your head?

If you can't remember where your mind was during the activities of your day, you aren't alone. Nor are you the only person whose thoughts simmer in anxious negativity and pain much of the time. Some estimates suggest we have around 45,000 negative thoughts a day, which is about 80 percent of our total daily thoughts. Most of these negative thoughts are repeats from the day before, and the day before that, and so on. We are training our brains to dwell in distress.

Every day, we fall down the same mental rabbit hole, and quite often, that rabbit hole is a dark and painful place. Our thoughts send us on harrowing journeys through regret, guilt, shame, and self-doubt. They propel us to scary and unpredictable futures, and lead us through mental wastelands and mind-numbing reveries, as our thoughts drift into fantasy, fiction, and other nonsense.

We may not be consciously aware of the unpleasant odysseys our thoughts take every day, but we are aware of how we feel, if not directly, then through the symptoms and consequences of our feelings. We may notice stress, physical tension or pain, sadness, anxiety, or irritability. We might snap at our kids, be distracted and preoccupied with our spouse, or lose focus on an important project. Our behaviors starkly expose our emotions, sometimes in destructive or self-sabotaging ways.

Our thoughts, and the feelings those thoughts produce, create our realities. If most of our thoughts and feelings are negative, then much of life is as well. Our thoughts cause us deep suffering through emotional or physical pain, loss and impermanence, and ego attachments. However, this suffering is unnecessary. Why? Because most of our thoughts simply aren't real or true. They *feel* real because of the way we attach and react to them. Fortunately, we have the power to change our perceptions and end much of the suffering in our lives through the practice of mindfulness.

The purpose of this book is to give you some tools to win back control of your thoughts and emotions so that you can release anxiety and fear to enjoy a richer, healthier, more conscious life.

Peace of Mindfulness

You don't need to live in a monastery or go on a month-long retreat to practice these skills or enjoy the myriad of benefits they afford. You can live your life, manage your obligations and responsibilities, and maintain your daily activities with little or no real disruption to your routine. All you need is a commitment to mindfulness and an understanding of how to incorporate it into your day.

Many of the techniques presented here are quite simple and take very little time. Some involve more time and deeper instruction, but you will find they provide profound and abiding rewards. The exercises I cover in this book aren't the only methods for practicing mindfulness. In fact, as you'll learn, you can practice it in everything you do. Ultimately, it's up to you to decide how you want to make mindfulness a part of your life, but the practices outlined will help you get started and give you options to open your mind to mindfulness. Hopefully you'll come to see mindfulness as the only way of life.

Barrie Davenport

Chapter 1: What Is Mindfulness?

*"When you realize nothing is lacking,
the whole world belongs to you."*

~ Lao Tzu

Mindfulness is the intentional yet gentle effort to be present with experience in a nonjudgmental way. When you are mindful, you are right here, right now, with a conscious, purposeful awareness of the present moment. You're not dwelling in the past nor focused on the future—unless you are doing so with mindful intention. You are attentively immersed in the moment.

"The best way to capture moments is to pay attention," says Jon Kabat-Zinn, Professor of Medicine Emeritus and creator of the Stress Reduction Clinic and the Center for Mindfulness in Medicine, Health Care, and Society at the University of Massachusetts Medical School. "This is how we cultivate mindfulness. Mindfulness means being awake. It means knowing what you are doing,"

When you practice mindfulness, you're not only aware of the present moment, but you are also in a state of emotional non-reactivity. Whether your experience is good or bad, pleasant or unpleasant, or simply neutral, you don't judge the experience. If you do judge it, then you simply observe your thoughts with a friendly curiosity and release them. They are clouds that float in and out of your awareness without erupting into thunder storms. You don't get upset or bothered if the experience isn't pleasant or not what you want. You simply accept whatever arises in the moment. Although mentally you might know an experience is positive or negative, emotionally you are balanced, poised, and in a calm place of equanimity.

Equanimity is a higher state of happiness than the situational elation or pleasure we experience in day-to-day life. It is steady and long-lasting, not based on the dualities of good or bad, pleasure or pain, happy or sad. Rather, it is contented non-attachment based on acceptance of what is happening in the present moment—a state of mind that affords a broader perspective of reality. Says Vietnamese Zen Master Thich Nhất Hạnh, "You climb the mountain to be able to look over the whole situation, not bound by one side or the other." The ego disappears, and you are able to see how the events occurring on the surface of your life are only as relevant as you believe them to be.

A common misconception is that the equanimity found in mindfulness is simply indifference. In fact, equanimity is a blissful state that provides an unshakeable freedom of mind not bound by the suffering of attachment to thoughts and feelings. It is an underlying peace that is detached from the push-pull drama of our longing for happiness. Through acceptance of what is, we realize gratitude for all things, good and bad. We come to this place through the regular practice of mindfulness.

Does that sound possible? Can you really be present in every experience as it occurs? Can you really prevent your mind from careening off into the past or future, as much as you might desire to be in the now? Does anyone have the self-control to view thoughts and events with equanimity, free from the ego and without emotion or judgment?

The answer is no and yes. Mindfulness is a practice, not a destination. The journey of daily practice *is* the destination. As with any practice, the more you work at it, the more proficient you become. Even so, very few people can achieve a constant state of mindfulness, or even experience it most of the time. Unless you are a monk or hermit, you have work and responsibilities that force distraction and pull you out of the moment.

As Jack Kornfield, one of the leading Buddhist teachers in America, reminds, "We all know that after the honeymoon comes the marriage, after the election comes the hard task of governance. In spiritual life it is the same: After the ecstasy comes the laundry." In other words, intense mindfulness practice must give way to the distractions and obligations of daily life. In fact, he believes we need to "get back down into the messy business of life" in order to integrate what we learn during our times of mindfulness.

Mindfulness practices like meditation do require time for practice, just like exercise or any other skill you're learning. A standard meditation practice is somewhere between thirty and forty minutes a day. Some monks and meditation experts meditate for several hours a day. But as you'll learn through this book, meditation isn't the only path to mindfulness. It can be practiced in a variety of real world situations, using many different methods. You can enjoy mindfulness for just a few minutes at a time and still reap the emotional, psychological, spiritual, and physical benefits.

As we experience the messy business of life, our moments and hours of mindfulness will stay with us, helping us learn new ways to be aware and enjoy the world around us, in good times and bad. It reminds us to savor every moment of life rather than rushing through it or getting lost in longing and suffering for what isn't real. The seismic shift in our perspective and perception of life that mindfulness provides is just one of the many benefits of the practice.

Chapter 2: The Benefits of Mindfulness

"The practice of mindfulness begins in the small, remote cave of your unconscious mind and blossoms with the sunlight of your conscious life, reaching far beyond the people and places you can see."

~ Earon Davis

The practice of mindfulness is so much more than just calming yourself down after a stressful day or refocusing your attention away from life's distractions. Mindfulness is a *way of life* that elevates your *quality* of life. It improves your mental and physical health, and fundamentally changes your outlook and view of yourself, your experiences, and even time itself. It helps you understand, tolerate, and regulate your emotions in healthy ways, and teaches you how to alter habitual responses as you make conscious choices about how you think and act. By slowing your racing thoughts, you can break free of limiting and self-sabotaging behaviors.

Mindfulness allows us to experience life as we live it and embrace the world directly through our five senses. We recognize the thoughts we are having, taste the food we're eating, and feel the wind on our skin. This in-the-moment experience of ourselves and the world allows us to cultivate gratitude, compassion, and self-knowledge. It also extends time in our perceptions, as we don't waste as much of it lost in thought or focused on the past or future. When every moment is truly "lived," then time tends to disappear.

Dr. Ellen Langer, a renowned mindfulness expert, experimental social psychologist and Psychology Professor at Harvard University, and the author of the groundbreaking book, *Mindfulness*, has researched mindfulness for more than thirty-five years, and knows the profound impact of mindfulness on success, health and well-being. She is convinced that all of our suffering in every aspect of our lives comes from *mindlessness,* and we lose ourselves when we identify with our thoughts. "We suffer from an illusion of certainty and would prosper from realizing that since everything is always changing and everything looks different from different perspectives, this 'certainty' is mindless and robs us of control," says Langer.

Study after study supports how profoundly the mindfulness impacts every aspect of our well-being and changes our experience of life.

Here are some of the benefits the practice of mindfulness provides:

Mindfulness reduces mental rumination and over-thinking.

Rumination and over-thinking cause anxiety, stress, and agitation and can lead to depression. Research studies support that practicing mindfulness helps you "stay out of your head" with over-thinking. In a study by Chambers et al. (2008), twenty people with no previous meditation experience participated in a ten day intensive mindfulness meditation retreat. The group reported significantly higher mindfulness, less rumination, and fewer symptoms of depression than the control group.

Mindfulness reduces stress.

The same study revealed that practicing mindfulness can decrease the levels of the stress hormone cortisol. Says University of California post doctoral researcher for the study, Tonya Jacobs, "This is the first study to show a direct relation between resting cortisol and scores on any type of mindfulness scale." This is one of many studies supporting the positive impact mindfulness has in relieving stress.

Mindfulness improves memory.

Practicing mindfulness has been shown to dramatically improve focus, memory, and reading comprehension. It reduces mind-wandering, thus improving performance. Studies of students who practice mindfulness show they perform better on tests than those who don't. Researchers at Massachusetts General Hospital revealed in a study that regular meditation (a mindfulness practice) causes the brain's cerebral cortex to thicken. The cerebral cortex is responsible for higher brain functions like memory, concentration, and learning.

Mindfulness helps with emotional reactivity.

The stressors in our day-to-day lives and relationships make it difficult to maintain emotional control. Often our feelings burst out in reactive ways like losing our temper, having an outburst of tears, or speaking out before thinking. Mindfulness practices help us become less emotionally reactive and respond to stressful situations in calmer, healthier ways. In another study (Ortner et al., 2007), researchers showed how people who practiced mindfulness meditation were able to disengage from emotionally upsetting pictures and focus better on a cognitive task, as compared with people who saw the pictures but did not practice mindfulness meditation.

Mindfulness promotes cognitive flexibility.

Cognitive flexibility is the ability to combine knowledge and experience in new ways and to apply thinking to situations one has not previously encountered. One study (Siegel, 2007) found the practice of mindfulness meditation allows people to develop self-observation (observing the self without judgment), which disengages the automatic neural pathways created by prior learning and develops new neural pathways to allow present-moment input to be integrated in a new way. It helps our thinking to be less rigid and more creative.

Mindfulness builds happier relationships.

A University of North Carolina study of "relative happy, non-distressed couples" revealed that couples who actively practiced mindfulness saw improvements to their relationship happiness. They also enjoyed healthier levels of "relationship stress, stress coping efficacy, and overall stress." The practice of mindfulness allows us to be present with our partners, to be less emotionally reactive with them, and to more quickly overcome stressful situations in the relationship.

Mindfulness helps tamp down anxiety and fear.

Mindfulness practices help reduce the amygdala—the fear center of the brain. The practices can increase the rational brain, or prefrontal cortex, to promote a calmer, steadier brain. When you detach from your anxious thoughts and feelings and observe them without judgment, they lose much of their power.

Mindfulness improves sleep.

Stress is one of the most common causes for insomnia and sleep problems. Mindfulness techniques promote calm and reduce ruminating and anxiety that can disrupt sleep. A University of Utah study confirms that mindfulness meditation practices help us get a better night's sleep. According to study researcher Holly Rau, "People who reported higher levels of mindfulness described better control over their emotions and behaviors during the day. In addition, higher mindfulness was associated with lower activation at bedtime, which could have benefits for sleep quality and future ability to manage stress."

Mindfulness promotes mental health.

University of Oregon researchers found that integrative body-mind training—which is a meditation technique—can actually result in brain changes that may be protective against mental illness. The meditation practice was linked with increased signaling connections in the brain, something called axonal density, as well as increased protective tissue (myelin) around the axons in the anterior cingulate brain region.

Mindfulness offers pain relief.

A variety of studies support mindfulness practices as a tool for relieving and coping with chronic pain. With mindfulness, rather than focusing on how much we want the pain to disappear, we notice our pain with curiosity and without judgment—as negative thoughts and judgments exacerbate pain. Mindfulness gives us a more accurate perception of pain, and reduces the secondary suffering that comes with evaluating and worrying about pain. In one study on the impact of mindfulness on pain, reported in the April 6, 2011, issue of The Journal of

Neuroscience, researchers saw a 40 percent reduction in pain intensity and a 57 percent lessening of pain unpleasantness with the participants who practiced mindfulness meditation.

Through my own mindfulness practices, I have experienced every one of these benefits personally. I have used mindfulness to cope with and reduce anxiety, worry, and depression. During post-operative recuperation, I've used it to manage pain and the frustration of recovery time. I regularly practice mindfulness when going to sleep and notice I fall asleep much more quickly. When I practice mindfulness techniques in my daily life, I feel more content, calm, and emotionally balanced. I'm happier in my relationships and view the world and my experiences with a more positive perspective when I take the time to meditate or use other present moment techniques.

One of the readers on my site, "Live Bold and Bloom," shared his experience with practicing mindfulness and how it's impacted his life:

> *"My wife started talking about mindfulness in the work she was doing with troubled children in the education system. The results sounded fascinating. I also read a book called The Emotional Life of Your Brain. From there my wife and I enrolled in a mindfulness course with the intention to teach and use it in the work we do as coaches and mentors.*
>
> *Since starting the course and having read many more books and articles my approach to life has changed from being a stressed, frustrated worried about the future type person who often over reacted and worried.*

I have always been a driven person who has experienced many things in life. Lifelong learning has always been my mantra until the good experiences dried up and life turned to disaster in many areas. Financial ruin, marriage breakdown and loss of job turned my life upside down.

The reclaiming of an abundant life has been supported by mindfulness. Relearning the ways to judge less, react differently, be in touch with life instead of living on autopilot has given a whole new meaning to life, my relationship, employment, and rebuilding an abundant life."

~ Wayne, Brisbane, Australia

The practice of mindfulness takes focus, commitment, and consistency, but remember, it is the *practice* that's your destination—not the perfection of the practice. Awareness of its powerful benefits is the first step toward embracing mindfulness as part of your daily life. In the next chapters of the book, I'll discuss some specific mindfulness practices and how you can incorporate them into your day.

Chapter 3: Mindful Breathing

"Breathing in, I calm body and mind. Breathing out, I smile. Dwelling in the present moment I know this is the only moment."

~ Thich Nhất Hạnh

Do you remember your last breath? I bet you're aware of the one you just took after reading that question. The average person takes over 20,000 breaths a day, and unless our attention is drawn to our breathing for some reason, we aren't aware of most of those breaths. Although it's essential for our survival, breathing isn't something we give much thought to.

Breathing is important for two reasons: it supplies our bodies and organs with the oxygen necessary for survival, and it rids our bodies of waste products. Oxygen is essential for our brains, nerves, glands and internal organs. Without it, we would die within minutes. If the brain is deprived of oxygen, it can damage other organs and systems in our bodies. Lack of oxygen is a major cause of heart disease, strokes, and cancer.

We are mostly unconscious of our breathing, and therefore we don't recognize when we're breathing improperly. In fact, you may not realize there is a proper and improper way to breath. Is there something more than just sucking in air and releasing it? Although breathing is managed in the unconscious, at any moment we can take over and consciously change how we breathe. Our modern lifestyles make conscious breathing more important than you can imagine.

Unfortunately, we are sedentary most of the day, so there is less need to breathe deeply, the way our ancestors did in order to hunt, gather, farm, and perform other manual labor. Sitting behind our desks or slumped on the couch watching TV, we have developed a habit of short and shallow breathing. When we're in a hurry and rushed, our breathing follows suit with quick, nervous breaths. When we're stressed, anxious, or focused on a problem, our bodies contract, and we bend forward, with our heads down, arms together, and muscles tensed. All of these postures constrict breathing. Sometimes when we're absorbed with stress and worry, the muscles that move the thorax and control inhalation and muscular tenseness clamp down like a vice to restrict exhalation, and we forget to breathe altogether.

So what's wrong with shallow breathing? A lot. These puny breaths make us fatigued from the decreased blood circulation and the decreased availability of oxygen for the blood. Shallow breathing causes us to lose some of the function in our lungs because the lungs don't get enough exercise. When we don't have sufficient oxygen, and we aren't expelling enough carbon dioxide, we build up toxins in every cell of our bodies. Oxygen starvation also leads to premature aging, reduced vitality, and a weaker immune system. With shallow breathing, we use only about a tenth of our lung capacity—which is enough to survive, but not enough for a high quality of life and a high resistance to disease.

The key to improving your breathing and reaping the health benefits as a result is paying attention to your breathing and becoming mindful of improving how you breath.

You can begin by taking these steps:

1. Take note of your breathing regularly. Just become aware of how you are taking in air throughout the day.

2. Sit up straighter, stretch, become aware of where you are tensing your body.

3. Breathe through your nose. The nose has defense mechanisms that prevent impurities and excessively cold air from entering the body. It also can detect poisonous gases that could be harmful. Pathogens can enter the lungs through mouth breathing—so keep your mouth closed and let your nose do the work.

4. When you inhale, push your stomach forward gently, and breathe through as though you are filling your stomach. This is called abdominal breathing.

5. When you exhale, breathe out slowly, and gently allow your stomach to return to its normal position.

6. Notice the difference between shallow breathing (which stops at the chest) and abdominal breathing. Abdominal breathing fills the lower lobes of the lungs, and it massages the abdominal organs by the movements of the diaphragm.

In addition to making these changes in your regular breathing style, you can further increase the benefits of mindful breathing by practicing a few minutes of deep or complete breathing every day. The complete breath, which is practiced in yoga, involves the entire respiratory system and employs all of the muscles.

Here are some simple instructions on deep breathing:

1. Sit in a meditative position, like the lotus position, or in a chair with your spine straight.

2. Inhale slowly until your lungs are filled to capacity.

3. At the end of the inhalation, pause for a count of two.

4. Exhale slowly, smoothly and completely. Pause at the end of the exhalation as well.

When you first begin, don't take too full a breath at once. Start by breathing to the count of four, pausing for the count of two, and exhaling to the count of four.

During the first week, don't take more than five or six deep breaths at one time as this could cause hyperventilation.

With practice, you will enlarge your lung capacity and be able to inhale more air than you have previously.

Breathing with Intention

In addition to becoming more mindful about *how* you breathe, you can also use breathing as a tool for mindfulness. Using the proper techniques, conscious breathing reduces stress and promotes relaxation of the mind and body. Slow, deep, rhythmic breathing causes a reflex stimulation of the parasympathetic nervous system, which results in a reduction in the heart rate and relaxation of the muscles.

Also, oxygenation of the brain tends to normalize brain function, reducing anxiety and stress levels. As the sixteenth century yogic sage Yogi Swatmarama reminds, "When the breath wanders the mind also is unsteady. But when the breath is calmed the mind too will be still, and the yogi achieves long life. Therefore, one should learn to control the breath." But don't just take an ancient yogi's word for it. Research reported in the November 28, 2005, issue of *NeuroReport* confirms that when mindful breathing is used to facilitate meditation, areas of the brain associated with attention and processing of sensory input grow larger. This phenomenon is particularly profound in older people, as it triggers the reverse of the typical thinning of grey matter as we age.

When you use breathing as a mindfulness tool, each breath becomes an object of concentration that draws us inward. Says Abbot George Burke, the founder and director of the Light of the Spirit Monastery in Cedar Crest, New Mexico,

> *"Rather than disperse our consciousness through objects that draw us outward, away from the center of our being, we can take an object that will have the opposite effect, present it to the mind, and reverse our consciousness. That object is the breath, which is the meeting place of body, mind, and spirit."*

Bringing our focus intentionally to the breath, we ground ourselves in the present moment. Observing our breathing without reacting, but simply watching each breath as it happens without needing to change it, is the beginning of letting go of suffering.

The Practice of Mindful Breathing

Almost all meditation practices begin with focused breathing. Just the breathing itself will calm and relax you, even if you do it for just a few minutes.

Here's how to begin:

1. Sit upright in a comfortable chair or on the floor with your hands on your knees or thighs, palms up or palms down, or resting in your lap.

2. Turn your eyes downward and close them gently to remove any visual distractions, which reduces your brain-wave activity by about 75 percent, helping to calm the mind.

3. Close your mouth so all breathing is done through your nose, which also helps quiet the mind. Keep your jaw muscles relaxed so the upper and lower teeth are not clenched or touching one another.

4. Imagine you have a balloon in your stomach. Each time you breathe in, the balloon inflates. Each time you breathe out, the balloon deflates. (This is diaphragmatic or abdominal breathing.)

5. Begin breathing naturally, and after the out breath count one. Then breathe in and out again and count two. Keep breathing and counting on the out breath this way until you reach ten, then begin again with one.

Thoughts will likely come into your mind, and that's okay, as your mind always wants to produce thoughts. Simply notice the thoughts, and bring your attention back to your breathing.

Practice this for five minutes at first, slowly increasing your time.

When you first begin the practice of mindful breathing, you may notice you feel more anxious at first. You may need to take some deep cleansing breaths, or you might feel you're short of breath. Just stick with it a few more minutes, and soon your body and breathing will relax. Over time, you will notice you're able to stop counting and simply focus on your breathing. You and your breathing become one. You can always return to the count if you find your mind wandering or feel detached from your breathing.

You are not necessarily trying to reach some altered state through mindful breathing. You are simply reconnecting with your own immediate life force and experiencing every breath in a restful, calm state. You can practice mindful breathing anywhere, at any time. It is a great "mini escape" from your work day, and helps you release stress and tension throughout the day. It is also a peaceful way to end your day as you are lying in bed, preparing to fall asleep. You may find you fall asleep before you get through two or three ten-counts of breathing.

Chapter 4: Mindfulness Meditation

"Rest in natural great peace, this exhausted mind,
beaten helpless by karma and neurotic thought,
like the relentless fury of the pounding waves
in the infinite ocean of samsara."

~ Nyoshul Khen Rinpoche

Mindful breathing can be used any time of day as a means to relieve stress and feel more calm and centered, and breathing alone is an important and valuable mindfulness tool. But as I mentioned before, breathing is often the first step in meditation—a more profound and committed mindfulness practice. The practice of meditation is a way to transform your mind by creating a beautiful state of stillness, silence, and clarity for sustained periods. As you practice meditation, you come to recognize the patterns and habits of your mind, and learn to cultivate a calm and positive mental state through the cessation of mental chatter and an increase in focused awareness.

Meditation requires no money, no special equipment or clothing, and takes a relatively short amount of time, especially in light of the rewards it provides. Through meditation, you strive to completely let go of the hectic world around you, and to find freedom from the past and future in order to achieve a state of bliss. And as I outlined earlier, there are an abundance of physical and mental health benefits associated with meditation. These outcomes alone are compelling enough reasons to embrace a meditation practice. Additionally, many religious traditions like Buddhism see meditation as a way to end suffering, enhance love and compassion, gain insight and awareness, improve concentration, and ultimately reach a state of enlightenment.

However, you don't need to be Buddhist or have any religious affiliation at all to enjoy the benefits of mediation. Vipassana (or mindfulness) meditation, for example, can be taught and learned in an entirely secular way. Says neuroscientist and secularist speaker and author Sam Harris, "The goal is to awaken from our trance of discursive thinking—and from the habit of ceaselessly grasping at the pleasant and recoiling from the unpleasant—so that we can enjoy a mind that is undisturbed by worry, merely open like the sky, and effortlessly aware of the flow of experience in the present."

Meditation has been practiced for thousands of years in many religious and secular traditions, and there are dozens of different styles of meditative practices. However, most practices begin with the same simple steps—sitting quietly, calming your mind, and remaining detached from judgment. The key to finding satisfaction with any meditation practice is simply to practice. By making a daily commitment to meditation, you will improve your skills and discover increasing benefits which accumulate over time.

In an interview on the blog "Lion's Roar," Buddhist meditation teacher Joseph Goldstein describes the progression of a meditation practice:

"I think you could describe it in different phases. The first phase is just seeing that there is a technique— even one as simple as coming back to the breath— and practicing doing that. That's the hard work of meditation, coming back again and again and again.

The second phase is when the mind develops some concentration and there is stillness and steadiness and ease. It all flows by itself; there's not that same effort. That's a wonderful opening, because the meditation gets to be very enjoyable and is not a chore anymore. The mind/body feels very light and fluid and the thoughts are no longer predominant. They still come and go, but they don't have the same power to drag you away.

The third phase is building on that concentration and using it, developing insight into the actual workings of the mind. So it's not just abiding in the calm, but seeing and observing. You see the unsatisfying nature of arising phenomena, because they just all pass away, very momentarily. And you begin to see what in Buddhism is called the emptiness of self. Those are insights you begin to see with greater and greater clarity."

Although meditation is difficult in the beginning, you *will* make progress and will one day have a moment when you think, "Aha, this is what all the fuss is about." You will long for more and more of these moments and be inspired to go deeper into your practice. But for now, simply a willingness to try meditation consistently for a period of time is enough, and you will very quickly discover a peace that has always been available to you. "Meditation is not a way of making your mind quiet," says physician, author, and speaker Deepak Chopra. "It's a way of entering into the quiet that's already there—buried under the 50,000 thoughts the average person thinks every day."

How to Begin Your Meditation Practice

If you want to create a regular practice of meditation, you need to first prepare yourself, your schedule, and your space. You prepare yourself by making a commitment to the practice and sharing your commitment with others so you have a sense of accountability. You want to be in a positive state of mind, open to all outcomes and possibilities without preconceived judgments or desires, simply knowing the benefits of meditation will reveal themselves in time. However, remember the purpose of these early sessions is to train and quiet your mind, so enter the meditation understanding this as the goal.

Determine the time a day when you will meditate, and choose a time in which you can eventually work up to thirty minutes of meditation. But in the beginning, start with just five or ten minutes and increase your time slowly. You might try a meditation in the morning and one in the evening if possible. Find a space in your home that is peaceful and conducive to meditating. You might want to light some candles, dim the lights, and remove any distractions or possible noises. Let others in the house know you are meditating, and ask them not to disturb you.

Here are the basic steps for a meditation practice:

1. Sit comfortably either in chair or cross-legged on the floor with a cushion. Keep your spine erect and your hands resting gently in your lap. Don't recline as you

may fall asleep. Erect posture will help you stay alert and awake.

2. Close your eyes, or keep them open with a downward focused gaze, then take a few deep cleansing breaths—maybe three or four.

3. Notice your body and the feeling of your body touching the chair or the floor. Be aware of your body in the space around you.

4. Gradually become aware of your breathing. Notice the air moving in and out through your nostrils and the rise and fall of your chest and abdomen. Allow your breaths to come naturally without forcing them.

5. Allow your attention to rest in the sensation of breathing, perhaps even mentally thinking the word "in" as you inhale and "out" as you exhale.

6. Every time your thoughts wander (which they will do a lot in the beginning), gently let them go and return to the sensation of breathing. Don't judge yourself or your intrusive thoughts. Just lead your mind back to focused attention on breathing.

7. As you focus on breathing, you'll likely notice other perceptions and sensations like sounds, physical discomfort, emotions, etc. Simply notice these as they arise in your awareness, and then gently return to the sensation of breathing.

8. When you observe you've been lost in thought, detach yourself from the thoughts and view them as though you are an outside witness with no judgment

or emotion. Label them by saying, "There are those intrusive thoughts again." Then again, return your attention to the breathing.

Continue with these steps until you are increasingly just a witness of all sounds, sensations, emotions, and thoughts as they arise and pass away.

Taming the Monkey Mind

In the beginning, you'll find you must redirect your thoughts almost constantly. You will often get caught up in the past and future and feel frustrated with your inability to tame your thoughts. But with time and practice, it will become easier and easier to just be the witness to all thoughts and sensations and remain focused in the now. You will experience immense peace in shedding attachments to everything except the present moment.

When you are outside of meditation in normal life, you carry many burdens and stresses in the form of thoughts. It's like having an albatross around your neck you must drag with you everywhere you go. During meditation, you give yourself permission to remove the albatross and abandon the burdens. This creates the right attitude for freedom and joy in your meditation. As you begin your meditation, remind yourself to release and banish the past and future. This means you don't think about your worries, your work or family, your childhood, or anything in your recent history. During meditation, you become a blank slate with no past or future and no interest in the past or future.

I love the description Theravada Buddhist monk Ajahn Brahm uses on his website to teach students how to manage unwanted thoughts:

> "I describe this as developing your mind like a padded cell! When any experience, perception or thought hits the wall of the 'padded cell', it does not bounce back again. It just sinks into the padding and stops right there. Thus we do not allow the past to echo in our consciousness, certainly not the past of yesterday and all that time before, because we are developing the mind inclined to letting go, giving away and unburdening."

During meditation, it is common to anticipate and worry about the process of meditating or the possible outcome you will or won't reach. You also may fret over how long the meditation will take or the small pains or discomforts you're feeling. During the early days of meditating, you'll wonder if the effort is really worth it. You might think, "Nothing is happening here. This is a waste of time. I don't see the purpose of this." You will feel your mind is a wild monkey that can't be tamed. You might even have a moment of stillness of mind, and in your excitement start a commentary on the experience—which removes you from the present moment.

Rather than engaging in commentary with every thought or feeling, simply observe and direct your attention to whatever is happening in the moment. Then observe whatever comes up and go back to the moment, and so on over and over. If you redirect your attention to the moment after every observation, you don't have time to get lost in commentary. It is like redirecting a toddler back to his bed until he gets the message you mean it.

Even if you don't feel like you're making progress, you are. Just keep at it. Acknowledge that millions of practitioners can't be wrong about the rewards of meditation and stay committed, knowing you will improve. Just as you work for several weeks in your job before you get your paycheck, you must put in the time in meditation before you get the payoff. At some point, you will abide in silent awareness long enough to experience how sweet and blissful it is.

If you'd like to learn more about meditation, I'd recommend the books *Real Happiness: The Power of Meditation* by Sharon Salzberg; *How to Meditate* by Pema Chödrön; *Meditation for Beginners* by Jack Kornfield; and *8 Minute Meditation* by Victor Davich. You can also find many free online meditation courses and guided meditations.

Chapter 5: Creating Flow at Work

"When you work you are a flute through whose heart the whispering of the hours turns to music."

~ Kahlil Gibran

Meditation is an excellent mindfulness practice you can even use during your work day to return to present moment awareness and inner calm. You can simply close your door, turn off your phone, and enjoy a few minutes of peace and freedom from thought. But you can't spend your entire day in meditation, even if you'd like to. You do have a job to perform, and most jobs or work environments aren't designed to support sustained mindfulness—through meditation or even in our work.

There are people all around us, talking, interrupting, and pulling us into meetings and conversations. Phones are ringing, computers dinging, and we find ourselves juggling a bottomless pit of projects, tasks, and unexpected crises. At best, we skim the surface of our core responsibilities, with little time for brainstorming, creativity, or passion for the work we are doing.

There are certainly exceptions to this scenario, but even in the most laid-back work environments, we are still addicted to our smart phones and computers, which alone create more distractions in an hour than previous generations had in an entire work week. Having the time, inclination, or freedom to detach from these distractions and to focus intently on the process of your work seems like a luxury—or maybe an impossibility depending on the culture of your job.

Simply the awareness that we're so often distracted and disengaged on the job begs a deeper question —why do we work in the first place? Of course we need to make money and pay the bills, but most any job will allow us to do that to one degree or another. So ask yourself, why do you have *this particular* job? Why have you chosen the career field you are in? If you like your job and sought training and education in order to work in this field, then you must find some level of satisfaction and joy from the core responsibilities of your work. You chose it because it engaged and interested you, and perhaps you have a natural aptitude for it. However, if you don't like your job, or you took it out of necessity, then distraction and disengagement might be your preferred modes of operating at work, simply to escape the boredom or frustration. Many people experience this situation, and it is a soul-crushing way to live.

When we can't plummet into depths of joy in our work, either because we're constantly pulled away or there are no depths to savor, then we feel empty, agitated, and trapped. Your work should fill your cup, not deplete it. It should, at least much of the time, energize and absorb you so that in the practice of your work, you lose yourself. This experience of losing oneself is known as the "flow state"—when we are intently immersed in the task at hand. According to positive psychologist Mihaly Csikszentmihalyi, author of the book *Flow, The Psychology of Optimal Experience,* flow is "being completely involved in an activity for its own sake. The ego falls away. Time flies. Every action, movement, and thought follows inevitably from the previous one, like playing jazz. Your whole being is involved, and you're using your skills to the utmost."

During flow, all aspects of performance are incredibly heightened, especially creative performance. Researchers have found creativity is enhanced both in the moments of flow and for the long haul, even after the flow state has ended. This creative enhancement isn't an inconsequential byproduct of flow states. It is a quality that tops nearly every "most valuable skills" list for employees, executives, and CEOs in recent years. Creativity is a highly-regarded strength in any profession or industry.

If you haven't enjoyed a state of flow in the past, or you're not sure if you have, there are some specific elements that comprise it and lead to the experience. According to Csikszentmihalyi, the state of flow involves ten components (although all ten don't need to exist for flow to occur):

1. There are clear goals that are attainable, yet challenging.

2. You have strong concentration and focused attention.

3. The activity itself is intrinsically rewarding.

4. There are feelings of serenity and loss of self-consciousness.

5. You lose track of time or feel a sense of timelessness.

6. You receive immediate feedback.

7. There is a balance between your skills and the challenge presented.

8. You feel personal control over the situation and the outcome.

9. You lose awareness of physical needs.

10. You are completely focused on the activity itself.

Being in a state of flow is what I call "active mindfulness." You aren't quietly focused on breathing or deep in meditation, but you are fully entrenched in the present moment. You are cocooned in the activity you're performing, so much so that you and the work are completely united. The work can be loud or physical (playing the trumpet or building a table for example), but you are still practicing mindfulness because you're in the flow of doing or thinking. This active mindfulness is facilitated with the support and complicity of your brain.

Profound changes occur in normal brain function when you are in a state of flow. Brainwaves switch from the rapid beta waves of waking consciousness to the far slower alpha and theta waves. Alpha waves are associated with the day-dreaming mode, while theta waves appear during REM or right before we fall asleep, when thoughts and ideas combine in creative and radical ways. These states promote creativity by allowing us to easily use old thoughts and information to create something novel while in a relaxed state.

During flow, we also enjoy a temporary deactivation of the prefrontal cortex, the part of the brain that houses most of our higher cognitive functions and gives us our sense of "self." With the quieting of the prefrontal cortex, we also lose our inner critic—the little voice that tells us we're doing it all wrong. In addition, during flow states, we enjoy a huge cascade of feel-good brain chemicals, like norepinephrine, dopamine, endorphins, anandamide, and serotonin. These chemicals increase pleasure, focus, pattern recognition, imagination, and other creativity boosting abilities.

Create Flow

Clearly flow is the way to go, but how can we create flow during our hectic work days, and how, for those of us who don't like our jobs, can we create flow around tasks that we find boring at best and loathsome much of the time? Let's begin with finding flow in the work you enjoy. Remember, as Mihaly Csikszentmihalyi tells us, to reach that optimal level of flow, your skill level needs to be aligned with the activity or task, but with the activity being slightly challenging.

With that in mind, here are some steps for creating the mindfulness of flow during your work day:

Determine your most productive time of day.

For many people, it's first thing in the morning when you feel rested and energized. However, your most productive time might be when you have the least chance of interruptions or other obligations.

Create a specific goal.

Determine exactly what you want to work on and what you want to achieve. This should be a task or project that utilizes your skills in a challenging way. For example, if you are in marketing, it could be creating your yearly marketing plan, writing a proposal, or brainstorming a new campaign. Set loose parameters for how much time you wish to spend on this project, so you have the freedom for creative thinking without the pressure of required "productivity."

Remove all possible distractions and interruptions.

Even small distractions like a text coming in can break the spell of the flow state. Turn off your phone and shut down any unnecessary browsers or sounds on your computer. Put a "do not disturb" sign on your door. Find a quiet space—or if music facilitates flow for you, play some of your favorite music.

Focus on the process rather than the result.

In our productivity-oriented culture, we emphasize fast work, quick results, and multi-tasking. Success is equated with getting the most done in the least amount of time. During these self-created periods of flow, you want to do just the opposite. You want to allow yourself the freedom to enjoy and explore the process without worrying about the outcome. Not that you won't reach an outcome or eventually achieve a result, but that won't be your focus during this time.

Set a timer if necessary.

If you can't stay isolated in flow for unlimited amounts of time, set a timer to pull you back into the fray when you need to. Most of us don't have the luxury of endless amounts of unscheduled, uninterrupted time. Your goal is to carve out as many of these flow times during your work week as possible. You will find by giving yourself these mindful times of flow, you are more engaged, creative, and productive in your work overall. Ironically, because you are energized and relaxed, you often get more done than you would by rushing or multitasking.

Flow When You Hate Your Work

Now let's address those situations when you don't like your work, or your skills and aptitudes are poorly matched with your job. Is it possible to create a state of flow in these circumstances? It can't happen as easily or naturally as it does when you're doing work you enjoy—but it is possible. In fact, creating flow in the face of boredom, anxiety, or apathy is a great goal to strive toward in order to help you cope and find some pleasure and peace as long as you stay with the job.

Here are some ideas:

Make exit-planning a flow activity.

If you're in a job that's not right for you, planning your exit strategy can give you a sense of control and hopefulness. Maybe you know what you want to do, or maybe you're still trying to figure it out. Either way, it takes some research, preparation, and analysis to get the ball rolling and to begin the shift. Rather than fretting about all of the potential roadblocks, allow yourself to start with a vision and figure out how to work toward that vision without judgment or doubt.

Create a list of actions you need to take to begin your exit plan. Then set aside thirty minutes to an hour a day to work toward your dream. Follow the flow steps outlined previously as you work on your plan. Remember, enjoy the process without focusing on the outcome. Enjoy dreaming, planning, and researching a new life for yourself, even if you can't make a change in the short term.

Chop wood, carry water.

There is a Zen saying, "Before Enlightenment chop wood carry water, after Enlightenment, chop wood carry water." In the early days of the Zen monasteries, monks had to perform basic tasks in order to keep things running. They couldn't sit in meditation all day if they wanted to eat and survive. Thus the practice of mindfulness while doing chores came into practice. Rather than resenting wood chopping or water toting, these tasks became opportunities for being present.

Most people wouldn't think of chopping wood or carrying water as their life passion or the work they love. If you don't like you're job, every task feels like chopping wood. However, you have a choice about how you wish to approach the work you disdain. Begin to notice the frame of mind you bring to your work. Do you approach your job as if it were a nuisance or a source of discomfort? Do you detach from work so that you are filled with resentment or worry? Rather than choose these mental paths, why not be more fully present in your work? Why not practice mindfulness in even the most mundane tasks?

I know when you feel trapped, unappreciated, or poorly matched with your job, the last thing you want to do is focus more intently on your work. However, you can approach your work with the same sense of equanimity you seek in all mindfulness practices. Rather than mentally and emotionally resisting the work, be fully alert and awake with every action you take.

Notice your thoughts as you work, which may continue to be negative—but rather than identifying with the thoughts, simply observe them without judgment, and let them pass. Then refocus on the task and do it as if it's the most important task in the world. In fact, go a step further and feel gratitude for all the circumstances that put you where you are at the moment.

Seek out the gems.

Even in a job you hate, there are always a few things you enjoy. It's just that the bad things tend to overshadow the good. Think about everything you do in your job, and isolate a few activities you enjoy or could enjoy if you didn't feel so bad about the entire job. Set aside a time of day you reserve for these gems, if that's possible. Do a mindful breathing exercise before you approach these activities to release as much stress or negativity as possible. Then perform the tasks following the flow steps outlined previously. Allow yourself to see the good in this work in spite of the bad in the rest of your job.

When we open awareness to the tasks in our jobs, or any part of our lives, they become less burdensome. We can be in the moment, and we don't feel so compelled to watch the clock. Whether your work is fulfilling or boring, bring all of yourself to it, and you'll find joy and peace you didn't know existed. You'll also be in a better frame of mind to seek out new opportunities and approach your work more creatively.

Chapter 6: Drinking Tea with Mindfulness

"Drink your tea slowly and reverently,
as if it is the axis on which the world earth revolves—
slowly, evenly, without rushing toward the future."

~ Thich Nhất Hạnh

A cup of tea. Say those words to yourself, and imagine holding a warm cup of tea in your hands. The words and vision alone are soothing and comforting. Recently I watched a drama series in which the very British characters consistently announced they'd "put the kettle on" after every uncomfortable or disastrous situation. It seems tea is the panacea for all that ails us. It's not just soothing, but it has many medicinal and healing properties as well.

For hundreds of years, tea has been used as an alternative medicine to treat everything from depression to cancer. Different varieties of teas are used for a wide array of ailments. Studies show some teas may help with cancer, heart disease, and diabetes, as well as encourage weight loss; lower cholesterol; and bring about a good night's sleep. Purists consider only green tea, black tea, white tea, oolong tea, and pu-erh tea the real thing, all which contain unique antioxidants called flavonoids. Flavonoids fight against the free radicals that contribute to cancer, heart disease, and clogged arteries.

The History of Tea

Tea was discovered in China sometime before 1000 BC and was used primarily for medicinal purposes. During the Tang Dynasty, tea spread to Japan by Japanese priests studying in China, and when Japan adopted Zen Buddhist beliefs, the Japanese tea ceremony was created. In the 1500s, the renowned tea master, Sen No Rikkyu, incorporated the ideas of rustic simplicity, morning ritual, and self-honesty into the tea ceremonies. The traditional Japanese tea ceremony has since evolved into a spiritual experience that embodies harmony, respect, purity and tranquility.

If you are a tea drinker, perhaps you drink tea as a stimulant to wake you up in the morning or afternoon. Or maybe you know about the medicinal benefits and consume it as part of a healthy diet. Sometimes I drink a cup of tea on a cold, winter afternoon to warm up. Most of us don't think about drinking tea as a form of mindfulness. When we're drinking it, we are usually doing something else at the same time—watching TV, working, or sitting at the computer.

In his book, *Anger: Wisdom for Cooling the Flames,* Vietnamese Zen teacher, Thich Nhất Hạnh, writes about how distracted we are when we normally drink tea:

> *"When you drink tea in mindfulness, your body and your mind are perfectly united. You are real, and the tea you drink also becomes real. When you sit in a café, with a lot of music in the background and a lot of projects in your head, you're not really drinking*

*your coffee or your tea. You're drinking your projects;
you're drinking your worries. You are not real, and
the coffee is not real either. Your tea or your coffee
can only reveal itself to you as a reality when you go
back to yourself, and produce your true presence,
freeing yourself from the past, the future, and from
your worries. When you are real, the tea also
becomes real and the encounter between you and
the tea is real. This is genuine tea drinking"* (pp. 43–
44).

Once you examine the medicinal and ceremonial history of tea drinking, it's easy to see how tea is a perfect vehicle for mindfulness. Although you can mindfully drink any beverage, tea affords a combination of physical sensations and health benefits that align beautifully with peace, purity, and present moment awareness. It's hard to create that combination with a diet Coke or a glass of tomato juice.

Chinese tea sage and "Tea God" Lù Yǔ (733–804), and author of the *The Classic of Tea,* honed his tea drinking methodology over many decades. In his book *The Way of Tea: Reflections on a Life with Tea (2010),* author Aaron Fisher explains Lù Yǔ's method:

> *"Lu Yu spoke of nine ways that man must invest
> himself completely in tea, which were:*
>
> *He must manufacture it.*
>
> *He must develop a sense of selectivity and
> discrimination about it.*
>
> *He must provide the proper implements.*

He must prepare the right kind of fire.

He must select a suitable water.

He must roast the tea to a turn.

He must grind it well.

He must brew it to its ultimate perfection.

He must, finally, drink it" (p. 164).

Lu Yu's ritual reflects the ancient Taoist practices of creating a deliberate immersion in nature, as the tea preparation includes the basic elements of water, wood (tea leaves and fire wood), fire, metal (the cooking brazier), and earth (the pottery cup). The tea ritual allowed people to connect with the primordial forces of the universal Tao, and by managing these forces through tea preparation, Lu Yu suggests we are reminded of man's civility and our ability to rise beyond the natural forces. Thus we are able to bring more peace and equanimity to our lives in spite of misfortune and suffering.

Your Personal Tea Ceremony

Unless you develop a keen interest in traditional tea ceremonies, you likely won't have the time or inclination to sit over the brazier in your back yard with your hand-selected tea leaves, mindfully roasting the leaves, grinding them, and brewing your tea. But you can certainly create your own mindful ritual around brewing and drinking tea in the comfort of your home, with modern appliances and store-bought tea. You can create this ritual as a deliberate, active meditation to break from the stress and adrenaline rush of daily life and enjoy a few moments of respite and peace. A tea ritual is something you can practice alone, or it can be shared as a way of being present with friends or your partner.

Says Thich Nhất Hạnh in *Anger: Wisdom for Cooling the Flames:*

> *"Tea meditation is a practice. It is a practice to help us be free. If you are still bound and haunted by the past, if you are still afraid of the future, if you are carried away by your projects, your fear, your anxiety, and your anger, you are not a free person. You are not fully present in the here and the now, so life is not really available to you. The tea, the other person, the blue sky, the flower, is not available to you"* (p. 44).

Here are some ways you can create a mindful tea ritual for yourself:

Select your cup.

Choose a cup or mug that feels good to you. Spend some moments choosing just the right cup. Hold the cup in your hands. Look at the shape, color, and design. Then set it down on the counter, ready to receive the tea. Don't drink from a paper cup or a chipped or broken cup.

Select your tea.

Tea bags are fine, but you might consider purchasing a few varieties of loose leaf tea to brew. Pull out several boxes or tins of tea, and smell each one. Inhale the scents deeply with your eyes closed, and allow each scent to "speak" to you. Which tea matches your mood or state of mind? Select your tea and place it in a teapot, cup, or strainer.

Boil water.

It might be quicker to microwave your water, but instead boil your water in an open pot or pan. Stand over the water and watch it heat up and boil. Watch as the steam rises and the bubbles form in the pan. Practice mindful breathing as you watch and wait. Don't busy yourself with other tasks or distractions.

Pour the water.

When the water boils, slowly and carefully pour the water over the tea leaves or tea bag. Watch as the leaves swirl and the water begins to change color as the tea infuses it. If you are using a tea bag, dunk the bag several times slowly.

Watch and wait.

Allow the tea to steep for three to four minutes, as you sit beside the cup and practice mindful breathing. Lean over the cup and allow the steam to warm your face and the scent of the tea to fill your nostrils.

Drink the tea.

Before you take the first sip, bring the cup to your lips and again feel the steam and notice the complex aromas. Take a sip as though you were tasting tea for the first time. As the flavor meets your taste buds, notice your reaction and feelings. Notice the sweetness or bitterness. Notice the delicacy or robustness. Hold the tea in your mouth for a moment and then swallow it reverently. Hold the cup in your hands, feeling the warmth of the cup and enjoying the sensations of that first sip. Continue to take sips like this, slowly and thoughtfully.

Offer gratitude.

As you drink, offer gratitude for the tea and your experience of the tea. If you are with someone else, offer gratitude for that person and for sharing tea with them. Notice everything around you, and offer gratitude that you are in this space, safely and reverently drinking your tea.

Wash your cup.

When you finish your tea, hand wash your cup and replace it where it belongs. Put away your tea things, then close your eyes and breathe slowly for two or three counts of ten. You are ready to resume your day.

Tea drinking is mindful and pure in its simplicity, yet can be a complex and enlightening experience. Try to practice the ritual a few times a week for ten to fifteen minutes, or longer if you have the time. If you are interested in trying loose leaf teas and different varieties of tea, take a look at the Teavana website (teavana.com) or peruse your local tea shop or grocery story and try some.

Chapter 7: Visualization and Guided Imagery

*"Surely there is grandeur in knowing
that in the realm of thought, at least,
you are without a chain; that you have the right to
explore all heights and depth;
that there are no walls nor fences, nor prohibited places,
nor sacred corners in all the vast expanse of thought."*

~ Robert G. Ingersoll

The 2014 men's final at Wimbledon was one of the most exciting tennis matches I've ever seen. The match pitted Roger Federer, winner of seventeen Grand Slam titles and crowd favorite, against Novak Djokovic, winner of seven Grand Slams. It was an epic match, with constant long volleys between Roger and Novak and several tie breaks, ultimately going to five sets. After nearly losing to Novak in the fourth set, Roger made an amazing comeback with a seven to five win. But in the end, Novak Djokovic took the fifth set six to four to win the Wimbledon title.

Just after the win, Novak was interviewed about the game and how close he came to winning in the fourth set. The interviewer asked how he was able to pull himself together when it appeared Federer (who is notoriously calm under pressure) was about to come back strong after being on the brink of defeat. Novak said that during a bathroom break, he used visualization, mindfulness, and positive self-talk to boost himself mentally and maintain the focus he needed to ultimately win the game. In fact, he used these techniques off the court as well to help him become the number one tennis player in the world.

In his book, *Serve to Win*, Novak says he uses mindfulness exercises like visualization to overcome self-doubt and recover more quickly from mistakes. It's also helped him become one of the greatest comeback players of all time. Novak says by practicing mindfulness meditation, he now simply notices negative thoughts and allows them to pass by. He is able to focus fully on the present moment, noticing any physical pain or negative emotions without getting tangled up in his thoughts. He credits his success as world class athlete to the mental toughness fostered by mindfulness, visualization, and positive affirmations.

Olympic swimmer Michael Phelps, the most decorated Olympian in history, has been using visualization since he was seven years old. During the Olympics and before any race, he visualizes every minute detail of his performance, and credits visualization for his competitive edge.

> "Before the (Olympic) trials I was doing a lot of relaxing exercises and visualization. And I think that that helped me to get a feel of what it was gonna be like when I got there. I knew that I had done everything that I could to get ready for that meet, both physically and mentally," says Phelps.

Visualization has been part of elite sports for decades. Al Oerter, a four-time Olympic discus champion, and tennis champion Billie Jean King, were among those using it in the Sixties. Many of us first noticed the impact of visualization on athletic performance in the Eighties when Russian researchers studied it with their Olympians. Their research revealed that athletes who spent 25 percent of their time engaging in physical training and 75 percent of their time mentally training had more success than those who spent 100 percent of their time physically training. Of course the Russian method for visualization required very detailed visualizations, performed frequently and consistently.

Today visualization is an essential tool in nearly every serious athlete's arsenal for peak performance and success. Even the Seattle Seahawks football team relied on it to win the 2014 Super Bowl, using their own in-house psychologist to facilitate visualization before athletic practices and games.

Visual imagery is effective at enhancing performance because when you imagine yourself performing perfectly, and you do this consistently and in detail, you create strong neural pathways in your brain, just as if you had physically performed the action. Because the brain tells the muscles how to move, these neural pathways result in more precise, stronger movements which are reinforced by gains made in actual physical practice.

Amazingly, visualization alone can sometimes facilitate change in the body without physical movement involved. In a study published in 1996 in the *Journal of Sport & Exercise Psychology,* researchers found that just imagining weight lifting caused actual changes in muscle activity. Other research has supported the findings that mental practice is almost as effective as physical practice in certain activities.

Visualization doesn't just enhance athletic performance. Mental imagery can be used in daily life and on the job to relieve stress and performance anxiety, enhance preparation, and add more power to your physical and mental efforts. Visualization has been shown to impact motor control, attention, perception, planning, and memory, priming your brain for success in whatever you want to accomplish. You can practice it to "set" and mentally strengthen intentions for future goals and desires.

For those who are coping with illness or pain, visualization provides both relief from suffering and enhances a sense of personal control over one's health. Simply the act of visualizing, which requires mindfulness, concentration, and creativity, frees the mind from mental commentary about the health issue and quells the anxiety and fear associated with these thoughts.

There is much debate in the medical community about whether or not visualization can actually "cure" certain diseases and ailments like cancer. The American Cancer Society provides an overview on their website of the use of imagery for cancer patients and the studies that have been conducted related to it.

Here are their comments:

> "A review of 46 studies that were conducted from 1966 to 1998 suggested that guided imagery may be helpful in managing stress, anxiety, and depression and in lowering blood pressure, reducing pain, and reducing some side effects of chemotherapy. Another review in 2002 noted that imagery was possibly helpful for anxiety, as well as anticipatory nausea and vomiting from chemotherapy."

They further state that some studies suggest visualization can directly affect the immune system. However they caution, "Although one uncontrolled, exploratory study suggested that guided imagery could improve survival for people with cancer, available scientific evidence does not support that these techniques can cure cancer or any other disease." There are no large-scale studies proving visualization can treat or cure diseases, but there are many studies showing that your mind does have a profound impact on your body. Feelings of stress, your own self-perceptions, and your general attitude all have been shown to impact physical health.

If you have a lot of stressors, poor self-esteem, and a negative outlook, you are at higher risk for certain health problems. Visualization and guided imagery (which is simply visualization guided by another person or a recording of another person) can be used to address stress and negative thinking, so you are in the right frame of mind to make healthy, positive choices and prevent chronic stress.

As a mindfulness practice, visualization synthesizes the body and mind, harnessing creative imagination to facilitate peace of mind, relaxation, happiness, enhanced motivation and confidence, and other positive mental, physical, and emotional changes. Mental imagery is a practice you can apply in a variety of situations in your daily life to help you shift away from anxiety, longing, fear, or confusion by focusing your thoughts on desired, positive outcomes—as though you were enjoying those outcomes in real time.

In his book, *Creative Visualization for Beginners*, Richard Webster shares a story about Walt Disney and his use of mental imagery to support his desire to create Disneyland.

"Walt Disney is an example of someone who believed in creative visualization and used it to create his entertainment empire. He called the process "imagineering." When you visit Disneyland or Disney World you are seeing examples of "the dream that you wish will come true."

Many years ago, I heard a story that I like to think is true. Apparently, years after Disneyland and Disney World were completed, someone said to Mike Vance, the Creative Director of Walt Disney Studios, "Isn't it a shame that Walt Disney didn't live long enough to see this?" Apparently, Mike Vance replied, "But he did see it. That's why it's here." Walt Disney may well have been the world's greatest creative visualizer" (p. 2).

As with meditation, visualization helps you train your mind—but you are training it with specific, detailed instructions rather than seeking freedom from all thought. It is a means of imprinting your mind with an outcome so that your brain chemistry supports your actual efforts. You may have your own Disneyland you want to create, or you may simply want to improve a small situation in your life.

Here are some examples of how you might use visualization in your daily life as a mindfulness tool:

1. You wake up in the morning feeling stressed about a meeting at work with a new client. You visualize the entire meeting from beginning to end proceeding exactly the way you want it to go. You mentally review every detail from the moment you walk in the

door until the end of the meeting, as though it were happening in present time.

2. You're feeling nervous about a doctor's appointment for a symptom you've noticed. You first visualize the symptom and the part of your body that's bothering you, and you mentally surround it with a white, healing light. You "see" the symptom relaxing and your body releasing tension and stress. Then you visualize yourself feeling calm and confidently walking into the doctor's office with the sense that all is well. You see yourself leaving the office with complete and total relief and calm.

3. You've been feeling restless and frustrated at work and know you're not in the right job. But you aren't sure how to leave or find something better. You visualize yourself in a new work environment feeling happy, fulfilled, and excited every day, doing exactly what you'd love to be doing. You see yourself entering the office with joy, and you feel the feelings of satisfaction and engagement in your work. You see yourself opening an envelope with your paycheck, and it is the exact salary you want.

4. You're driving home from work and worried about an argument you had with your spouse on the phone earlier in the day. You feel stressed and anxious that you'll have to face an unpleasant scene when you get home. You visualize the entire encounter with your spouse from the moment you walk in the door. You are calm, centered, and able to communicate with your spouse easily and with love. You are

quickly able to come to a resolution and enjoy the evening together.

In each of these situations, and in any others you encounter in daily life, you can use visualization to control and manage your scattered and anxious thoughts. You create the present moment as a palette for a future you desire. Even if the ultimate outcome doesn't exactly match your imagery, you have governed your thoughts and clarified your desires. In the present moment, you've given yourself the gift of self-mastery, positive expectation, and peace of mind.

How to Visualize

Here are some steps for a personal visualization you conduct yourself:

Step 1: Create a specific goal or outcome.

Before you visualize what you want, define your goal or desired outcome. It needs to be specific, detailed, and achievable. Rather than saying, "I want a loving relationship with my wife," your goal should be, "I want to spend more time talking and touching. I want to do something fun and playful every day. I want us to feel safe sharing our vulnerabilities." Your goal also must be something in the realm of possibility for achievement. If you want to be a professional dancer, but you're forty years old and have never danced, the odds of success are slim.

Step 2: Define the actions for achievement.

Brainstorm and write down all of the actions you'll take to achieve your goal. For Michael Phelps, these actions include every stroke in the pool, every kick, and every turn at the wall. If your goal isn't athletic, you still need to visualize successfully mastering every step along the way. Outline these steps before you begin your visualization practice so you know exactly what you want to visualize yourself doing.

Step 3: Carve out the time.

Determine when you want to practice your mental imagery. First thing in the morning and before you go to bed are great times to practice, but you may also want to visualize before a specific event or effort toward a goal. As you get closer to reaching your goal, or if you have a big milestone to accomplish as part of the goal, you may want to increase your visualization efforts.

Step 4: Set the mood.

Every time you practice visualizing, be sure you are in the right space and frame of mind to do this mental work. If possible, visualize in a quiet room, and remove all possible distractions (phone, computer, etc.). Sit comfortably and take a few deep breaths, then mentally see a blank slate in your mind. From that blank slate, begin your visualization. If other thoughts or feelings pop up, gently release them and turn your attention back to your visualization, just as you would do with meditation. If you are agitated or emotionally upset, wait until you are calm to begin visualizing.

Step 5: Begin with the end.

Each time you visualize, picture the ultimate goal first. In your mind's eye, see yourself reaching the goal or living the desired outcome. Visualize it as if it were a movie, and you are the lead character. Picture exactly what you are doing, how you look, who is around you, where you are, and how you feel. Get as specific and detailed as possible. Allow yourself to feel the feelings of success as you visualize it. Experience it as though it were happening right now.

Step 6: Visualize the actions.

After you visualize reaching your goal, then mentally rehearse the details of each action you need to take. If your goal is physical, like weightlifting or playing tennis, then visualize each movement. However, if your goal has many mental steps and actions involved in making it happen (like finding a new job), then visualize successfully completing the actions required for the day or week. Break the goal down into smaller actions to visualize.

Step 7: Support your mental efforts.

You can boost your visualization practice by creating physical reminders that you've already achieved your goal. If possible, take a picture of yourself acting as if you've crossed the finish line. For example, if you want to work for a specific company, take a photo of yourself in front of the building. Post the photo where you can see it every day. You could also create a vision board by cutting out photos from magazines reflecting the success you want to achieve and pasting them to a poster board. Keep the vision board where you can see it daily.

Step 8: Set an intention.

Rather than hoping or dreaming about success, set an intention about the goal you want to achieve. When you intend to do something, there's a mindset of determination and finality. Notice the difference between the statements, "I hope to become president of the company," and "I intend to be president of the company." When you talk to yourself or others about your goal, be mindful of the language you use. Choose words of intention and inevitability rather than leaving the mental door open for anything other than complete success.

Visualization and Guided Imagery for Emotional Healing

Visualization and guided imagery are also excellent methods to support emotional healing. This healing might include stress relief, reprieve from symptoms of depression or anxiety, improvement of self-esteem and confidence, or grief management. You can visualize scenes and situations in which you experience the state of mind and feelings you want, and you can envision scenes in which you release feelings you no longer want.

For example, when used as a relaxation technique, you might imagine a scene in which you feel completely calm and peaceful, free to let go of all tension and anxiety. First select a setting that is calming to you—like a beautiful beach, a grassy meadow, or a cozy room with a fire. You can perform this visualization exercise on your own in silence or with a facilitator or audio recording guiding you through the imagery. You might use a sound machine or download sounds on your phone or computer that match your chosen setting— like ocean waves or falling rain.

Find a quiet place to begin your visualization, and try to perform it while sitting rather than reclining so you don't fall asleep. Create the setting you want with music, a guided audio, or recorded sounds. Then do a short breathing exercise before you begin. Start by imagining your peaceful place, and mentally picture it as vividly as you can. Make note of everything you see, hear, smell, and feel. Visualization is most effective when you incorporate as many sensory details as possible.

If your relaxing place is the beach for example, you might . . .

See yourself walking through the sand to the edge of the water.

You feel the warm sand as you walk, and then the cool water as it laps over your feet.

You smell the salty air and hear the seagulls cawing and children playing in the distance.

A wave splashes your face, and you get a taste of the salty water.

You feel a light, cooling breeze, as well as the sun warming your back.

You notice a feeling of complete peace and relaxation wash over you.

If you wish to release negative feelings about yourself, boost self-esteem, or you want to heal from grief or emotional pain, you might visualize placing all of your sad or negative feelings in a balloon. Label each feeling and place it gently in the balloon, and then release the balloon and watch it float gently into the sky and out of sight. Follow this imagery with a scene of yourself feeling happy, self-assured, free from guilt or shame, and living the way you wish to live. Again, be as detailed as possible, using all of your senses.

Whatever you wish to heal or achieve through this process, use your imagination in advance of your visualization session to determine the specific scene and the mental process you will follow, rather than trying to make it up as you go. You can even record a guided visualization for yourself and listen to it to lead you through the visualization you create. The sound of your own affirming voice is powerful.

Visualization is a creative method for being fully present while defining and picturing the future. It is carefully crafted, highly focused daydreaming with specific intent. The process can bring you peace of mind, afford motivation, and create a positive attitude. But be careful not to become too attached to or dependent upon visualization to "make things happen." Try not judge the process, fret about the outcome, or blame yourself if the visualization doesn't "work."

It is much more prudent to view visualization as a mindfulness exercise rather than a "law of attraction" tool. There is nothing magical or mysterious about visualization. Like all other mindfulness practices, it is a way of being present, training your mind, and rewiring your brain. The changes that occur in your brain can have many benefits, including supporting your real-world efforts at positive change and reaching your goals. You will always gain something positive from the practice of visualization, but there's no guarantee your visualization will become reality. As with any other skill, the more you practice it (using plenty of detail and all of your senses) the more benefits you'll realize—especially the joy of exploring your limitless capacity for creative imagination.

Chapter 8: Positive Affirmations

"Any thought that is passed on to the subconscious often enough and convincingly enough is finally accepted."

~ Robert Collier

Over thirty years ago, I came across the book *You Can Heal Your Life*, by Louise Hay. The book is about self-healing through the use of positive affirmations that correspond with different illnesses and ailments. I was intrigued by the book at the time, but also skeptical about Ms. Hay's claims that our thoughts and lack of self-love contribute to disease and that using positive affirmations can heal us. Although I understood how affirmations could support positive thinking, I didn't believe they could change the cells and chemistry in my body.

There's no scientific evidence that affirmations cure disease, but science does support the power of positive affirmations when it comes to changing our brains and feeling better about ourselves. Affirmations are basically a form of auto-suggestion, and when practiced deliberately and repeatedly, they reinforce chemical pathways in the brain, strengthening neural connections, in the same way neural pathways are formed with mental imagery. Says David J. Hellerstein, M.D., a Professor of Clinical Psychiatry at Columbia University, "In brief, we have realized that 'neuroplasticity,' the ongoing remodeling of brain structure and function, occurs throughout life. It can be affected by life experiences, genes, biological agents, and by behavior, as well as by thought patterns."

Neuroscience now proves that our thoughts can change the structure and function of our brains. (If you want to learn more about this fascinating science, check out the book *The Brain That Changes Itself: Stories of Personal Triumph from the Frontiers of Brain Science* by Norman Doidge, M.D.) By practicing positive thought patterns (affirmations) repetitively, we create neuroplasticity in the area of the brain that processes what we are thinking about. The more we flood our brains with affirmations, the thicker and denser the associated brain regions become.

Affirmations are short, powerful positive statements about yourself, your abilities, or your goals and intentions. They are spoken in the present tense, as though they are your current reality. The goal of affirmations is to change the way you think and feel about yourself, and as a result change your reality as your subconscious mind accepts these statements as truth. When affirmations are combined with other mindfulness practices like meditation, visualization and flow activities, you are creating even stronger neural connections, which eventually translate into more consistent feelings of positivity, motivation, and well-being.

Dr. Sonja Lyubomirsky, a professor in the Department of Psychology at the University of California, Riverside, and author of groundbreaking book, *The How of Happiness*, conducted and published a study in the January 2014 issue of *Personality and Social Psychology Bulletin* on self-affirmation and how it impacts psychological well-being. Her findings confirm the power of affirmation for improving self-image, meaning, and the sense of flow.

Here's what she reports in her study:

> *"Finally, because self-affirmation prompts people to reflect on the values and experiences most important to them, it may also encourage them to engage in activities that are congruent with those values— activities that are absorbing and enjoyable, also known as flow activities (Csikszentmihalyi, 1990). Flow experiences are rated as intensely positive, and people who frequently experience flow report relatively more life meaning and more positive states overall (Csikszentmihalyi, 1999; Rogatko, 2009). Little is known about methods to enhance flow experiences, but one experiment found that practicing optimism successfully increased flow (Layous, Nelson, & Lyubomirsky, 2013). Accordingly, we predicted that self-affirmation would boost the flow component of eudaimonic well-being."*

The practice of using affirmations can help you overcome negative thinking, limiting beliefs, and self-sabotaging behaviors. You can use them for a variety of goals or intended changes in your personal or professional life. If you have a social event, presentation, or meeting, it's good to use affirmations in the hours beforehand to boost your confidence and reinforce your skills. If you're feeling insecure, unproductive, or stuck, affirmations can jumpstart a change in your emotions to improve your self-image and any self-destructive behaviors. Affirmations can return you to mindful presence, as you focus your thoughts and emotions on specific words that are packed with meaning and intention.

67

In general, affirmations . . .

- should be short and positive statements;

- target a specific belief, goal, or behavior you're struggling with;

- should be credible, believable, and based on a realistic assessment of facts;

- should be formed in the present tense, as if they're already happening;

- should be repeated several times a day to flood your brain with positive thought;

- must be thought or spoken with feeling and real intention.

When practicing affirmations, choose one or two to focus on for several weeks. When you begin your affirmation practice, close your eyes, calm yourself with breathing for a minute or two, and say the affirmation in your head several times, focusing intently on the words and feelings you experience. Be completely present with the affirmation. Then speak the affirmation out loud in a strong, confident voice. Do this several times a day and before you go to bed. To add more power to the affirmation, write it down several times in a journal first, and then speak it out loud.

Here are some examples of positive affirmations for various situations you can use for yourself or as a template for writing your own:

I feel joy and contentment in this moment right now.

Peace of Mindfulness

My partner and I communicate openly and resolve conflict peacefully and respectfully.

I speak confidently and joyfully, and communicate my thoughts with ease.

I easily find solutions to challenges and roadblocks and move past them quickly.

I feel powerful, capable, confident, energetic, and on top of the world.

I have now reached my goal of _____ and feel the excitement of my achievement.

When I breathe, I inhale confidence and exhale timidity.

I live in the present and am confident of the future.

I love change and easily adjust myself to new situations.

I approve of myself and love myself deeply and completely.

I fully accept myself and know that I am worthy of great things in life.

I choose to be proud of myself.

I am completely pain free, and my body is full of energy.

I sleep soundly and peacefully, and awaken feeling rested and energetic.

My work environment is calm and peaceful.

I release past anger and hurts and fill myself with serenity and peaceful thoughts.

I am focused and engaged in the task at hand.

I am grateful for this moment and find joy in it.

I release the past and live fully in the present moment.

I am free of anxiety, and a calm inner peace fills my mind and body.

All is well in my world. I am calm, happy, and content.

Please note that if your self-esteem is low or you are coping with depression, anxiety, or any other mental illness or disorder, repeating positive affirmations you don't really believe about yourself or your abilities might not lead to the change you want. If you are affirming, "I am beautiful and lovable," but you feel you are neither, your subconscious will know you aren't being honest. In these situations, craft your affirmations with realistic honesty, while affirming the possibility for change.

For example, if you don't feel beautiful and lovable, your affirmation might be, "Today I acknowledge my limiting beliefs, and I am learning to love and accept myself more and more each day." As an intelligent person, you know when an affirmation feels phony or unattainable. Sometimes you need to first affirm small steps before you move big mountains.

Affirming positive statements about yourself and your abilities is a worthwhile practice on its own. But I've found affirmations to be particularly powerful when used with meditation and visualization. If you are trying to be present and aware for an extended period, or at least for an amount of time longer than it takes to speak or write an affirmation, then combining these techniques can create a potent and compelling mindfulness experience.

Affirmations with Meditation

When you combine affirmations with meditation, you clear mental space and create fertile ground for your affirmation to take hold in your psyche. It's often difficult to unhook from the busyness and mental distractions of everyday life in order to practice affirmations effectively. When your head is filled with mental chatter, and you feel agitated or adrenaline fueled, you might approach affirmations as just one more item to check off your to-do list—rather than being fully present and engaged with them.

For one of your daily affirmation sessions, consider combining it with a short meditation. Start by deciding on the affirmation statement you will use. It's good to create a short affirmation that works well with in/out breathing and that you can remember easily. I like to make a positive statement on the in-breath, and when applicable, make a release statement on the out-breath.

Here are some examples . . .

I breathe in joy . . . I breathe out frustration.

I embrace peace . . . I release tension.

I earn plenty . . . and release all debt.

I embrace forgiveness . . . and let go of anger.

Or you can make each statement positive, like these . . .

I am completely healthy . . . and filled with energy.

I am now seeing . . . the man of my dreams.

I speak with ease . . . and feel totally confident.

I eat healthy foods . . . and lose ten pounds.

Before you begin mentally saying your affirmation, just meditate for five or ten minutes so you can be completely relaxed and have a tranquil state of mind. Once you feel relaxed and have quieted most of the mental chatter, begin using your affirmation. On the in-breath, mentally say the first part of the affirmation, focusing on the words and the meaning of the words. Try to *feel* you are actually breathing in the concept you're speaking, if that works for your affirmation. Feel that you are breathing in joy, peace, confidence, etc., and that you are releasing anger, tension, self-doubt, and so on.

As with any meditation, if your mind drifts or you get distracted, gently bring yourself back to the breathing and affirmations. If you notice yourself detaching from the words and just mechanically thinking them, take a cleansing breath, and reengage with what you are saying. At the end of the meditation, speak the affirmation out loud, followed by the declarative statement, "This is happening for me right now."

If you wish, you can also record yourself saying the affirmation, using the same rhythm of your breathing during meditation. Some people can better focus on the affirmation when they listen to it rather than speaking it to themselves. If this works better for you, be sure you use a lot of energy and positivity while recording your affirmation; say it like you really mean and believe in it.

Affirmations with Visualization

Affirmations and visualization naturally work well together, as words automatically create pictures in our mind's eye. There are two ways you can combine affirmations and visualization. First, when you create a scenario you want to visualize, write an affirmation that encapsulates the visualization.

For example, if you visualize yourself getting the new job you want, your affirmation might be, "I confidently interview for a position as senior VP of sales, and I am offered the position at the salary I want." Speak and write the affirmation several times with emotion (like you are telling someone about it after it's happened). Then visualize the entire scenario as outlined previously. Once you finish the visualization, take a few deep breaths, and speak the affirmation several more times.

The second technique is to begin with the affirmation. When you speak and write your affirmations, take a few minutes more to visualize yourself taking the actions you're affirming—feeling the feelings and accomplishing the goals you define in your affirmation. Again, do this with emotion and attention, as though the affirmation has already occurred.

If your affirmation is, "I now speak confidently and joyfully, and communicate my thoughts with ease," then mentally see yourself in the setting where you are speaking, going through everything you want to say, smiling and speaking easily, and receiving positive feedback from your listeners. Even if your affirmation is an abstract concept, like breathing in peace or relaxation, you can still create mental pictures of this using whatever images suggest the concepts for you.

You might see yourself breathing in a white light or a warm sensation for example. Try to picture each part of your affirmation statement, even the parts where you release something. I like to picture putting beliefs or feelings I don't want into a balloon and letting it float out of sight. Try to choose positive, calming images rather than negative, destructive ones.

73

Practicing positive affirmations will help ground you in the present moment by intently focusing your attention and emotions on something you desire—but not as a future longing. Rather you are experiencing the present moment as the desired reality. Speaking and thinking your affirmations gives you a sense of creative control over your present experience, as well as contributes to positive life change by supporting new beliefs and motivating correct action.

In the same way reinforcing a new habit makes it easier to naturally follow through on the habit over time, using affirmations makes it easier to do what needs to be done to actualize your affirmation. Affirmations help carve new neural pathways to smooth the way for actionable life change.

Chapter 9: Mindful Fitness

*"Your mind, emotions and body are instruments and
the way you align and tune them
determines how well you play life."*

~ Yogi Bhajan

I think many of us have a love-hate relationship with exercise.
I'd put myself in that category. There are days I enjoy going out
for a run, and other days you have to pry me out of my chair
with a crowbar. Of course there are some athletes who can't
wait to hit the gym or run the next triathlon, but they are the
exception rather than the rule. If the national the epidemic of
obesity is any indicator, there are far more physical activity
avoiders than fitness lovers—but it wasn't always this way.

Physical activity used to be part of daily life in agrarian
societies. Virtually all Americans were farmers and had to be
active all day in order to survive. Men hunted and farmed;
women gathered and cooked. No one was doing much sitting
around. The Industrial Revolution changed everything, as we
moved from hand production to machines. Over the last few
hundred years, we've become increasingly immobile at home
and work, especially in the last half-century, as technology
keeps us firmly planted in our swivel chairs and in front of

computers. Our fingers and thumbs are the only body parts that see regular movement.

Although we no longer live like hunter-gatherers, we still have hunter-gatherer genes. We still store energy in fat cells, but with more access to food throughout the year, we don't burn that stored energy the way our ancestors did. As a society, we eat more and move less. In fact, according to the US Centers for Disease Control and Prevention, 80 percent of Americans don't get enough physical activity, and more than a third of U.S. adults are obese.

Since daily physical activity is no longer a way of life, a regular exercise program is a necessity for health and longevity. A regular fitness program also has been shown to reduce stress and anxiety and lessen the symptoms of depression. But sadly, many people would rather sacrifice their mental and physical health than force themselves to exercise. Truthfully, exercise is uncomfortable and sometimes even painful. It takes a lot of time, effort, and determination to maintain a fitness routine, especially when we don't have an immediately compelling reason for physical activity (like putting food on the table).

Part of the problem is the mindset we have about exercise. We dread it and find a myriad of creative excuses to avoid getting our bodies moving. We look for shortcuts, quick solutions, and pain-free options. We make a yearly "resolution" to exercise, one that we end up breaking within a few days or weeks of starting. Then we feel guilty and lazy, which de-motivates us to try again. Perhaps guilt and fear aren't the best motivators for positive change anyway. What if we could change our feelings about exercise by changing the way we approach it? I know from personal experience it's possible to find joy in fitness by combining it with mindfulness. Moving your body is a perfect way to practice mindfulness, and mindful movement is the perfect way to practice physical activity.

Most of our conscious awareness seems to take place from the neck up. Our brains are housed in our heads, so it feels like we "live" at the very top of our bodies with the rest of us attached for the convenience of transportation and dexterity. Our head seems to be the captain of the ship, and that's why we so often got "stuck in our heads" through rumination and worry. But when you place your attention and focus on other parts of your body, you extend consciousness in a way that creates harmony and balance between body and mind.

Rather than approaching fitness as a painful necessity for your health, consider approaching it as another mindfulness practice—one that has the added benefit of making you fit and improving your overall wellness. Once you remove judgment, attachments, and fear from the equation, fitness can be something to look forward to rather than an obligation you dread.

You no longer anticipate the discomfort, think constantly about quitting, or judge your results. You simply engage in mindful movement, pushing yourself slightly to improve each time, while pay full attention to your body. There are many forms of exercise that work especially well with mindfulness. Before I review those, let me first outline the basics of creating and sustaining a mindful exercise habit.

How to Create a Mindful Fitness Habit

Even when you approach fitness as a mindfulness practice, you will still have goals related to your workout, especially if you're trying to lose weight, run a marathon, or simply work up to the minimal amount of exercise recommended by health professionals, such as the US Centers for Disease Control and Prevention. Creating any new habit, particularly a new fitness habit, requires learning a specific set of skills that I outline in detail in my book *Sticky Habits.* Here's a brief overview of how to approach a new habit so you don't give up too soon.

Start small. In order to establish a regular routine, begin with just five minutes a day for the first week. This might feel ridiculously short, especially when you are eager to get started, but don't break this rule. When you first begin, you want your new fitness habit to be so quick and easy that you can't make excuses to skip it. Increase the time slowly (by five minutes a week) over the next few weeks, until you reach your desired amount of exercise time.

Set a time/find a trigger. Determine the time of day you want to exercise. Find a time when you can increase your total fitness routine from five minutes to thirty minutes or an hour (or more if that's what you want). Perform your new exercise immediately after a trigger, which is a previously established habit that's automatic, like brushing your teeth, making coffee, or going to the bathroom. The trigger is your cue to begin your exercise program, so begin it immediately after the trigger.

Create a reward. Reward yourself immediately after you finish exercising. It can be anything that feels good and rewarding to you. You might put a gold star on your calendar, do five minutes of meditation, enjoy a piece of chocolate, or just sit outside and enjoy nature.

Set up accountability. Share your new fitness habit publicly by telling friends and family, announcing it on social media, or joining a forum. Report daily on your success or failure to perform your fitness habit. Knowing you must report your progress adds motivation to follow through.

These basics will help ensure you stay on track as you incorporate a regular fitness program into your schedule. If you falter or skip a few days, don't use that as an excuse to quit. Simply go back to five minutes (or the last amount of time you last worked up to) and begin again.

Now that you understand how to prepare for a successful habit, how do you choose a mindful fitness program? Truthfully, any form of fitness can be practiced mindfully. The key is to approach exercise in the same way you approach meditation or any other mindfulness practice, with an inward focus that extends to your physical form and movements.

These are some fundamentals for any form of mindful fitness:

1. Affirm and visualize your goal and performance.

Before you begin, create an affirmation about your ultimate goal. It might be something like, "I am now easily and effortlessly running five miles in thirty-five minutes." Then mental visualize exactly what you will do during your immediate practice. See yourself going through your entire workout, enjoying what you're doing, and performing optimally.

2. Notice your body.

As you begin and get warmed up, focus your attention on the placement of your body. Are you standing or sitting correctly? Are you moving your limbs properly? Is everything aligned as it should be? Notice how your body feels and any pain or discomfort. Without attaching to the feelings, simply identify them. "My feet are hurting. My back itches. It's hot out here."

For any pain or discomfort you feel, try not to resist or fear it, but rather breathe into it and mentally see it relaxing.

Mentally send consciousness and energy to whatever part of your body is performing the work of the exercise. If several parts are moving at once, spread the energy throughout your body.

3. Focus on your core and alignment.

Your core is the center of your strength and support for all movement. For your core to operate efficiently, your body must be aligned with your back straight, shoulders back, and head held high (unless the exercise calls for something else). Let your core do most of the work while your limbs are fluid and relaxed. Even if you're lifting weights with your arms or legs, engage your core to add power to your limbs. As you exercise, focus on engaging your core, and envision an imaginary steel rod keeping your body in proper alignment.

4. Focus on breathing, sounds, or a mantra.

Depending on your particular exercise, once you are in the groove of the movements, focus your attention on your breathing, the sounds of nature, or a mantra you repeat. If you are running for example, you could focus on the sound of your feet hitting the pavement. Or you could create a mantra or affirmation that matches your breathing pattern.

If you're strength training, vividly focus on the muscles you're training and the energy surrounding those areas. Follow your breathing, and breathe out as you lift or engage the weight, and breathe in when you lower it. Stay focused on your breathing, even in between lifts.

When thoughts try to intrude, simply return to mindfulness, or take a moment to return to your body to access how it feels and adjust or relax as necessary. Then go back to breathing or your mantra.

5. Listen to your body.

If you are relatively new to exercise, and you aren't in tune with the various pains and feelings in your body as you work out, then let your body be your guide in how hard to push yourself and how long or far to go. If you feel pain that seems excessive or unusual, then stop or do something different. Don't criticize or judge yourself for this. Part of mindfulness is paying attention to the messages your body is sending and then responding with loving kindness.

Says Danny Dreyer, founder of the mindful running practice, Chi Running,

> *"The presence that I build through Body Sensing allows me to hold a bigger picture in the back of my mind. This, in turn, helps me respond to each moment in a more accurate and appropriate way, because my mind is not perpetually being caught off balance."*

As your mind and body work together in harmony through physical movement, you'll often find yourself in the state of flow when time disappears. In fact, increasing your exercise time will be almost effortless. Since you won't expend energy on resistance, worry, or self-judgment, all of your efforts can go toward improvement, strength, body awareness, and self-acceptance. A calm, centered, non-resistant athlete simply performs better.

81

Mindful exercise allows your body to become an extension of your creative force and mental energy. If you are interested in an exercise program that offers more than just physical fitness, there are several options that intrinsically provide a deep connection between mind and body.

Here are some options you might consider in place of or in combination with more traditional fitness programs:

Yoga

The word yoga is a Sanskrit word, which is an ancient Indian language. It's derived from the word yuj, which means to yoke, as you'd yoke a team of oxen. This definition is often interpreted as meaning union, and yoga is said to unite the mind, body, and spirit. Yoga is about creating balance in the body through stretching and flexibility, and awareness in the mind through concentration on poses.

Yoga helps you:

- build strength

- increase flexibility and muscle tone

- enhance mindfulness

- encourage physical and mental balance

- develop proper body alignment

- reduce stress

- promote a sense of calm and peace

- increase lung capacity for better breathing

As with meditation, there are many styles of yoga practices, all with varying exercises, philosophies, and desired outcomes. Hatha yoga is the most widely-practice form of yoga, and is one of the six original branches of yoga. It uses movement and breath together to produce a "flow" of postures that lead from one to the next.

For the purpose of mindful fitness, yoga is a program of physical poses (asanas) designed to purify the body and provide physical strength and stamina. It works with the energy in the body, through pranayama or energy-control. Prana also refers to breath, and yoga teaches us how to use breath-control in order to still the mind and attain higher states of awareness. A beginning yoga class might include the following asanas.

Initial relaxation

At the beginning of the class, the student lies on his back in a relaxed pose while breathing deeply. The teacher will guide students through a relaxation exercise where students alternately tense and release various parts of the body. The combination of deep breathing and tension/release helps calm the mind and relieve tension in the body.

Sun salutations

The sun salutation is a sequence of twelve yoga positions performed at the start of every yoga class as a warm-up. Dozens of muscles are stretched and toned in this yoga exercise, as the sequence is performed several times.

Shoulder stand

The shoulder stand is an inverted pose that increases the blood supply to the brain, by lifting your legs perpendicular to the floor and resting your weight on your shoulders, neck, and head and supporting your back with your hands. It exerts a gentle pressure on the neck region, which helps regulate the functions of the thyroid gland (which governs metabolism).

Fish pose

With this pose, you stay flat on your back, and bring your feet together. With your arms straight by your sides, you tuck your hands in underneath your buttocks. Then you arch your spine, and tilt your head so that your crown rests on the ground, and hold the pose for thirty seconds. This yoga pose energizes the thyroid gland and enhances the flexibility of the upper back.

Forward bend

With this yoga pose, you inhale and take the arms up over the head and lift and lengthen up through the fingers and crown of the head. You exhale and slowly lower the torso towards the legs. Reach the hands to the toes, feet or ankles. This stretches the entire back of the body, increasing the flexibility of the lumbar spine and improving postural alignment. It also gives a nice massage to the abdominal organs.

Triangle pose

The triangle is a standing yoga pose with a sideways bending movement that simultaneously stretches, contracts and relaxes all major back muscles, and makes the spine more elastic. It also provides a deep stretch for the hamstrings, groins, and hips.

Final relaxation

Again the student lies on her back and is guided through active relaxation (tensing and releasing muscles), deep breathing and a visualization exercise to end the class.

In a typical class, the teacher may go through many more poses than just these, as there are hundreds of different poses. Any of these poses can be practiced for a few minutes during the day as a brief mindfulness practice to refocus your attention on your body and to relax and calm you. Please note that yoga isn't a cardiovascular fitness program, so it needs to be combined with another form of exercise to get your heart rate up. If you are interested in a regular yoga practice, I suggest you watch or practice a beginning yoga class online or register for a beginning class taught in your area. Once you become more advanced and learn a series of poses, you can practice at home on your own.

Ballet

Ballet did not begin as an exercise program. It is a form of artistic expression that has its beginnings in the courts of Europe for opera and stage performances. As it has evolved over the years, ballet has become more strenuous and physically demanding, requiring intense focus, discipline and stamina. However, more and more adults (men and women) are taking recreational ballet classes as a way of keeping fit, flexible, and mentally engaged.

There are amazing benefits to taking regular ballet classes:

Ballet sculpts and tones your body. The movements taught in ballet class are designed to create long and lean muscles without building up a lot of bulk.

Ballet promotes great posture. In order to perform the various positions, turns and combinations in ballet class, your body must be placed in correct posture and alignment. As a result of this very specific and repetitive training, you will continue to carry "ballet posture" outside of class.

Ballet promotes strength and flexibility. Ballet requires stretching and extending limbs and muscles, and holding these positions using the strength of core muscle groups. Stretching and strength exercises at the ballet barre are an important part of every ballet class. Over time, you will see tremendous improvement in strength and flexibility.

Ballet promotes stamina. Although ballet looks elegant and easy, it requires a great deal of strength and stamina. Repetitive movements, jumps, and dance combinations provide aerobic exercise that gets the heart pumping.

Ballet stimulates mental focus and discipline. In order to achieve correct positions and proper alignment, you must maintain a high level of concentration and body awareness. Also, the instructor gives a series of movement combinations (in French) that must be quickly memorized and repeated in the classroom. Ballet requires both mental and physical stamina.

Ballet encourages artistic expression, as it is an art form before it's an exercise practice. The technical aspects of ballet require discipline of the body and mind, but the artistic element of dance requires opening your heart and soul. Ballet is a way of expressing and communicating feelings, ideas and events. A ballet dancer enjoys moving to beautiful and inspiring music and expressing the emotions that the music evokes.

Ballet is for anyone. You can be a complete novice and walk into a beginning ballet class and reap great benefits from just one class. As with any exercise, you will get better with practice.

Tai Chi

Tai chi began in China as a martial art, but as it developed, it took on the purpose of enhancing physical and mental health. It is a series of low impact, weight bearing, and moderately aerobic movements that enhance physical and mental health. There are a variety of styles of tai chi, but they all involve slow, gentle movements, deep breathing and meditation—sometimes called "moving meditation." Tai chi is believed to improve the flow of energy in the body, leading to healthy living and providing a wide range of benefits.

A tai chi class might include the following:

Warm-up. Easy motions to help you loosen your joints and muscles and help you focus on your breath and body.

Instruction and practice of tai chi forms. Forms are sets of movements which may include a dozen or fewer movements. Long forms may include hundreds of movements. Focusing the mind solely on the movements helps produce a state of mental calm and clarity.

Qigong. This translates as "breath work" or "energy work" and consists of a few minutes of gentle breathing sometimes combined with movement. The idea is to relax the mind while mobilizing the body's energy. It may be practiced standing, sitting or lying down.

There are numerous health benefits to the practice of tai chi:

Tai chi improves balance, coordination, flexibility and strength. The Oregon Research Institute found that tai chi participants performed better at moderate to rigorous activities after six months of practice than non-participants.

Tai chi helps reduce pain and stiffness associated with conditions such as arthritis, osteoporosis, and fibromyalgia.

Tai chi improves the quality and length of sleep according to The Oregon Research Institute. The sleep benefits from tai chi are the same as those gained from drugs or cognitive behavioral therapy.

Tai chi strengthens the immune system, particularly against the viral disease shingles. Researchers have found that tai chi produces an immune response to shingles similar to that promoted by the vaccine for the virus.

Tai chi reduces stress. The practice of tai chi has a calming and meditative effect that reduces stress and anxiety.

Qigong

Qigong is a form of Taoist yoga. Taoism suggests that the health of the mind and body is dependent upon a clear, strong balance flow of qi or life force. The benefits of qigong extend to every physical system of the body, as well as the mental, emotional and spiritual aspects.

Qigong is an integration of physical postures, breathing techniques, and focused intentions. The practices of qigong can be classified as martial, medical or spiritual, but all styles have three things in common: they all involve posture (whether moving or stationary), breathing techniques, and mental focus.

There are a wide variety of qigong practices which can be very gentle, as with tai chi, or it can be extremely vigorous with styles such as kung fu.

The practice of qigong involves a moving meditation by coordinating slow flowing movement, deep rhythmic breathing, and calm meditative state of mind. A unique feature of qigong is the ability to train the mind to direct the body's energy, or chi, to any part of the body. The practice can relax the mind, muscles, tendons, joints and inner organs, helping to improve circulation, relieve stress and pain, and restore health.

Other benefits of qigong include:

- greater stamina, strength and vitality

- enhanced immune system

- lower blood pressure

- better coordination

- reduced stress and anxiety

To find a qigong instructor, you can visit the International Qigong Alliance online where they provide a directory of instructors. You can also find many videos online with instruction and exercises.

Whether or not you choose one of these mindful fitness programs, be aware that mindfulness can and should be incorporated into any exercise you choose. A quick Google search will show you how athletes and trainers are combining mindfulness with their particular sport or fitness program.

Chi Running, created by ultra marathon runner and coach Danny Dreyer, combines the principles of tai chi to make running easier, more efficient, and more enjoyable. Bodybuilder, meditation teacher, and author, Chris Willetts, has created Mindful Strength, a system of weight training that integrates mindfulness. Cyclists, rock climbers, and swimmers use mindfulness techniques for a more focused, productive exercise experience. Even the military is employing mindfulness-based fitness programs to help with stress resilience and peak performance.

Since fitness should be part of your life for your overall physical and mental health anyway, choose to practice your particular fitness program mindfully. Simply being more aware of your body, your breathing, and your surroundings will help you break free from your thoughts and focus more attentively on your performance and practice. You'll find more joy in your workout and see how the combined effects of mindfulness and movement reduce stress and energize you.

Chapter 10: Mindful Journaling

"A personal journal is an
ideal environment in which to 'become.'
It is a perfect place for you to
think, feel, discover, expand, remember, and dream."

~ Brad Wilcox

An old-fashioned pen and a blank sheet of paper are an invitation to freeing your mind, expanding your creativity, and finding inner peace. Daily writing, preferably writing by hand, is a mindfulness practice that has many unexpected rewards. It can help you process stress or frustration by getting it out of your mind and onto paper. It helps you order and clarify your thoughts, form ideas, define your perspective, and have more self-awareness.

When you are focused on writing, you experience that feeling of joyful "flow" when you lose track of time and get immersed in the process. As you write, you develop analytical skills, work through problems, and define your goals and dreams. Writing has even been shown to help us sleep better and is associated with improved mood, well-being, and lower stress levels and depressive symptoms.

Committing to a practice of daily journaling will help you harness the chattering "monkey mind" and detach from your thoughts and feelings as you release them on to your page. Says freelance writer Alan Furth on his blog, the written word "imposes a visual organization of human consciousness that contributes to a sense of being separate from the information transmitted through language." He further states, "This sense of distance and detachment strengthens our capacity to observe the world as an inherently external phenomenon." With detachment comes freedom, peace of mind, and expanded access to observation, interpretation, and creativity.

For the purpose of mindfulness, writing by hand with pen and paper (as opposed to writing on a computer) is the optimal way of reaping the greatest benefits from writing. Hand writing requires deeper thought while processing information and more focused attention, because you take longer to write by hand than you do typing. You also don't have the distractions of a computer when you write in longhand.

Says creative writer Lee Rourke in an essay for *The Guardian*,

> *"For me, writing longhand is an utterly personal task where the outer world is closed off, just my thoughts and the movement of my hand across the page to keep me company. The whole process keeps me in touch with the craft of writing. It's a deep-felt, uninterrupted connection between thought and language which technology seems to short circuit once I begin to use it."*

The act of writing helps the brain develop functional specialization that integrates sensation, movement control, and thinking. "Study after study suggests that handwriting is important for brain development and cognition," reports a 2010 article from *The Week*, citing a study from psychologist Virginia

Berninger of University of Wisconsin. She tested school-age children and discovered they generate more ideas when writing essays by hand than they do on a computer. The sequential finger movements involved in writing by hand activate multiple regions of the brain associated with processing and remembering information. You may be addicted to typing on a keyboard, but for your mindfulness journaling, allow your words to flow on real paper.

You don't need to be a professional writer or even a particularly good writer to enjoy the mindfulness benefits of daily writing. The point is to simply write and allow yourself to get absorbed in the writing. To make writing a daily habit, you can follow the steps I outline in Chapter 9 on creating a fitness habit, by starting small, creating a trigger and reward, and increasing your time slowly over several weeks.

Before you begin, buy yourself a nice journal or notebook (perhaps a bigger one for home and a smaller one to keep you your purse or pocket), and find a pen that feels good in your hand and writes smoothly. You might buy several pens to keep in different places. Set up your writing space exactly as you like it, with good lighting and a comfortable place to sit. You want your writing to feel like a meditation if possible, so create your writing space with that in mind.

In her beautiful book on creativity, *The Artist's Way*, Julia Cameron invites readers to the practice of daily writing through an activity she calls "Morning Pages." As she describes on her blog . . .

> *"Morning Pages are three pages of longhand, stream of consciousness writing, done first thing in the morning. There is no wrong way to do Morning*

Pages –they are not high art. They are not even "writing." They are about anything and everything that crosses your mind—and they are for your eyes only. Morning Pages provoke, clarify, comfort, cajole, prioritize and synchronize the day at hand. Do not over-think Morning Pages: just put three pages of anything on the page . . . and then do three more pages tomorrow."

Morning Pages is an excellent practice to begin your habit of daily writing and to discover how this practice allows you fall into a flow experience and detach from distracting mental commentary. Morning Pages is simply free writing with no particular agenda. You can write about your cat, the argument you had with your boss, what you see out the window, or any trivial subject you can think of. Or you can write about something you feel passionate about or that makes you angry or frustrated. This practice is a great way to rid yourself of mental clutter before you begin your day.

Passion Journaling

In addition to the free writing of Morning Pages, there are many other forms of journaling that invite mindfulness. I teach my life passion students to use journaling to help them on their journey of finding their passions. Passion journaling involves daily inner and outer awareness and chronicling observations and feelings. You pay close attention to how your life is unfolding from hour to hour, and then write down what you notice in order to find clues to your passion.

Peace of Mindfulness

Carry a small journal with you daily, and begin noticing daily experiences or situations that lead to feelings of . . .

- well-being or fulfillment;

- a sense of purpose, significance, or alignment with your values;

- being in the flow where time stands still;

- enthusiasm and joy;

- admiration or deep interest in someone or something.

These experiences or situations can arise during your work day, in interactions with loved ones, or during your non-working hours when you are engaged in a hobby or task. You can also explore these feelings when watching a movie or TV program, reading something in a book or on the Internet, or simply being outside in nature. The key is to pay attention. Be aware of what you are doing and how it makes you feel. If it makes the cut of the feelings listed above, then write about your experience in your journal.

You don't need to write a lengthy saga for each experience. Just outline the experience as soon as you can after the event, noting what you did and how it made you feel.

Here are a couple of examples from my own life:

> *I talked with my friend about the frustration she was having with her significant other. She openly shared her feelings with me and asked for my input. I summarized what I saw as the main issue, and she acknowledged that I nailed it and that no one else*

had seen the problem as clearly. That made me feel valued and significant. It supported my core value of serving others.

I cleaned up my office, clearing off my desk entirely, throwing away a bunch of papers, and prioritizing my work for the next few weeks. This made me feel productive and happy. While I was doing it, I was in that flow experience as I was concentrating on the decisions and activities involved.

The difficult part of this exercise is the constant awareness—paying attention to your feelings, identifying them, and associating them with the activity or experience you are having. But it is the most important aspect of this process, and that's why journaling about it is so vital. You are aware of these experiences when they are happening, and you relive them when you write about them. Both the initial awareness of the experience and your feelings about it, and the recounting of it in writing are mindful practices.

The experiences and feelings you journal about offer clues to your life passion. The times when you feel joy, flow, engagement, significance, purpose, admiration, and alignment with your values are snapshots of what you want more of in your life. In fact, some of these very experiences may ultimately be part of your passion.

Here are a few questions you can ask yourself to extend your awareness of the experiences:

Do any of the experiences you listed in your journal fit with one or more of your strong interests, your aptitudes, your core values, or potential passions?

Do you see correlations or obvious combinations between two or more of these experiences?

Do any of these experiences relate to how you envision a passionate career or hobby?

Which experiences do you find yourself intentionally repeating?

Which experiences created the most profound, memorable feelings?

When you have a moment to sit and think about these questions, make notes about your thoughts in your journal. Go back and review your journal entries regularly to look for patterns and repeat experiences. Work on your journal for several weeks—allowing yourself enough time to have a variety of experiences and situations to review. At the end of three or four weeks, take an hour or so with your journal and create a master list of experiences and the corresponding feelings associated with them.

Once you have this master list compiled, you will begin to pay more and more attention to situations in your life that fit in with this list. You can use your insights to brainstorm career opportunities or side gigs that might be your life passion. You may even realize that your life right now is filled with more passionate experiences than you initially thought. Focusing on the positive in life is a great exercise in shifting your attitude and detaching from looping thoughts and worry about your frustrations and unhappiness.

Gratitude Journaling

Another way to create mindfulness through journaling is to keep a gratitude journal. A quick search on Google will uncover study after study showing how gratitude markedly improves feelings of happiness and self-esteem. According to Sonja Lyubomirsky, Professor of Psychology at the University of California, Riverside and author of *The How of Happiness*, "By relishing and taking pleasure in some of the gifts of your life, you will be able to extract the maximum possible satisfaction and enjoyment from your current circumstances."

Sadly our brains are designed to remember more negative events and situations than positive. This is an "old brain" survival mechanism that ensures we don't make the same mistakes repeatedly—those mistakes that could have been life-threatening when we lived in the wild and needed to avoid wild beasts and club-bearing neighbors. Now our worries and negative thoughts are less life threatening but equally pervasive. Gratitude is a powerful antidote for the human brain's tendency to focus on the negative, and gratitude has been found to be very effective.

A gratitude journal is a rewarding and simple way to practice mindfulness while boosting your wellbeing. The journal is simply a daily record of people, events, feelings, and possessions in your life for which you feel grateful. It can include far more than the usual items on the tip of your tongue. In my own gratitude journal, I write about how thankful I am for my comfy bed, the owl that hoots outside my bedroom window at night, and the way warm, crusty bread tastes dipped in olive oil. Every nook and cranny of your life holds a gem you might take for granted, so be creative and thorough in your gratitude. Here are some additional thoughts about a gratitude journal:

Write first thing in the morning. Begin with some deep breathing to relax you and clear your mind. Then close your eyes and mentally say the words, "I am grateful for . . . ." Wait

98

expectantly for the ideas or images that come to mind, and then write them down. If nothing immediately comes to mind, then simply look around the room and make note of everything you feel gratitude for. Try to write more than a just a list—use expressive adjectives or adverbs to describe the person, situation, or thing. According to Sonja Lyubomirsky, depth more than breadth in writing about gratitude affords more benefits. Make note of your feelings about the items on the list. For example, you might say, "I am grateful for the warm sunlight streaming through my window and the way it brightens the room. It makes me feel comforted, happy, and peaceful."

Write before you go to bed. Before you go to sleep at night, do the same deep breathing exercise and mentally repeat the same words. Think about people, circumstances, and events you encountered during your day that you feel thankful for, and write these in your journal, just as you did in the morning. A good way to stimulate ideas is to think about what your life would be like without certain blessings. You may not feel immediate gratitude for your old clunker car, but how would you feel if you had no car at all? Include a statement of gratitude for a good night's sleep as an affirmation that you will sleep well.

Mix it up. If you find yourself writing about the same things over and over each day, then simply pick one gratitude item and write more in-depth thoughts about it. For example, you might write a few paragraphs about your spouse or child, remembering a specific scenario or moment that brings you joy and positive memories. Or you might write a descriptive paragraph or poem about something in nature and how it makes you feel. Be creative in how you journal your feelings of gratitude.

Focus intently. If you write in a gratitude journal regularly, you may find you start to just go through the motions and lose touch with the emotions involved. This defeats the purpose, as you've allowed distractions and your mental chatter to interfere with being fully present with the exercise. After you finish writing an item on your list or writing a paragraph about one particular item, close your eyes and intentionally savor the experience and feel the feelings of being truly, deeply grateful. See the item, event, or person as a priceless gift that has been given to you. Think about it the way a little boy who has never owned shoes might feel about getting his first pair ever, or the way a mother might feel upon seeing her son arrive home from a year serving in the military in a dangerous country. Sit with that feeling for a few minutes and just "soak" in gratitude.

Don't forget yourself. Be sure you include gratitude entries about yourself. Start by expressing gratitude to simply be alive and able to write in your journal. Express gratitude for your health, your five senses, your skills and abilities, your personality, your appearance (even if you don't like everything about it), your intelligence, your creativity, your ability to give and receive love—and anything else you can think of about yourself. You often take many things about yourself for granted, and mindfully expressing gratitude about these things will boost your self-esteem and confidence.

Meditation Journaling

Keeping a meditation journal is another powerful way to combine two mindfulness practices. After meditation, journaling about your session helps you have a better sense of what you experienced and how it impacted you. It gives you an accurate perspective on your practice. By taking a few minutes to journal immediately after you meditate, you can examine the experience with a fresh memory and the desire to learn and grow in your practice by chronicling what happens and how you feel about it. Over time you'll be more aware of your weaknesses and strengths, and have a more penetrating understanding of what you need to improve or focus on in your meditation.

Journaling will help you stay committed to your meditation practice. It serves as a silent accountability partner, sitting by your bed or on the table waiting for you to write about your daily practice. Says mental health advocate, blogger, and author Mark Freeman, "One of the benefits of keeping your journal is learning about the excuses you make to skip out on meditation. When your mind throws them at you in the future, you'll be better prepared to laugh at them."

Most importantly, a journal allows you to review your meditation experience and how it's changed over a period of time. You can clearly see the patterns your mind follows and how you've gained control over your thoughts and mental chatter. You may also come to recognize how certain distractions happen more or less often than you might think.

Chronicling your experiences with your meditation practice reveals how beneficial meditation has been for your state of mind, your stress level, and your overall feelings of contentment and inner peace. As you look back at your past meditation sessions, you can set goals related to your practice—what you need to work on, where you need more patience, persistence, or self-acceptance. Whatever changes you want to make with your practice, having clear goals will help you reach them. Just be aware that self-honesty and accuracy is important in your journal so you have a realistic picture of how you're progressing.

You can begin your journaling practice by allowing five minutes after meditation to simply write about your experience and how you felt about it.

Here's an example of what an entry might look like:

> *Meditated for fifteen minutes. Felt anxious and distracted at first. Kept getting distracted with thoughts about work. Eventually was able to focus on my breathing, but it felt difficult, and I really had to work to stay focused. Feel a little blue that it's not easier and more relaxing. I feel like I'm doing something wrong.*

It might help to have journal entry prompts when you first begin meditation journaling. Consider asking yourself these questions after each session and replying in your journal:

How long did you meditate?

How hard was it to stay with your breathing?

What distractions did you encounter?

How deep did you go in your meditation?

What impressions came to you?

How did you feel physically and emotionally?

What stopped you from going deeper or higher?

Consider writing only on the right side of your journal, leaving the left side blank so you can go back and make notes or include any additional thoughts that come up after the session. As you become more experienced with meditation and practice varying forms of meditation, you'll have more to write about and new and profound insights about your practice. In fact, as your meditation experience becomes more advanced and refined, your journaling might progress in an entirely different direction, mirroring the mental, emotional, and life changes you're encountering.

If you decide to keep a meditation journal, I strongly suggest you commit to writing in it after every meditation session so you can get the complete picture of your progress. If you only write in it occasionally, you won't have enough information to know what you need to work on and how far you've come. As you write in your journal regularly, you'll be amazed to see on paper how your struggles have diminished, your mind is calmer, and you feel more centered.

You might be interested in a community of other meditators who share their meditation experiences in an online journal. If this appeals to you, check out opensit.com. Although you won't have the benefit of writing your journal in longhand, you will enjoy sharing with a group of like-minded people and learning from their experiences and struggles.

Barrie Davenport

Chapter 11: Mindfulness as a Way of Life

"Life is available only in the present moment."

~Thich Nhất Hạnh

Sharon is a 41-year-old mom of three school-aged children. Since her oldest was born twelve years ago, she was able to stay home and take care of the house and kids. Her husband Matt had a demanding job with a bank that required he travel several days a week, so Sharon got used to handling all of the carpooling, housekeeping, and meal preparation.

Matt lost his job six months ago, and hasn't found another one yet. Sharon took on part-time work at the school to help make ends meet, but the rest of her schedule hasn't changed much. She's still taking care of everything at home so Jack can focus on finding work. Sharon feels anxious and overwhelmed most of the time. She wants to be strong for Jack and the kids, but she always feels like crying.

Max is CFO at a large construction company. He's been there for twenty-two years, ever since he worked construction there after college. Now he's making more money than he ever dreamed of, and he and his wife Sandy have a big house and two kids headed to college. Life would be great, except he's miserable in his job. For the last year, he can't sleep and feels generalized anxiety every morning. A few months ago, he thought he was having a heart attack on the way to work, but the doctor told him it was a panic attack.

Dewan is a high school basketball coach and PE teacher. He has to be at the school by 6:45 in the morning, and stays late to coach the team. He has a long commute, and often doesn't get home until after 8:00 in the evening. Being single, Dewan hasn't minded this schedule so much. But now his mom has cancer. He's an only child and his mom needs him. She's moved in with him, and he's trying to juggle his schedule so he can take care of her. He needs to quit the coaching work, but that's the only part of the job he really likes. He constantly worries about what to do and where his priorities should be.

Sharon, Matt, and Dewan live lives similar to most of us. They have good days and bad. They have the stresses and demands that come with the normal experiences of life. Even during the best of times, our lives are still harried and distracted with technology, work, and obligations that make us feel unsettled and agitated. Add a big life change or stressful event to the mix, and we might find ourselves flailing with debilitating anxiety. The interesting phenomenon about anxiety is that it's triggered by something that hasn't happened. Sharon feels anxiety about her future because Matt hasn't found a job yet. Max feels anxious because he looks ahead and sees a lifetime trapped in an unhappy job. Dewan is worried because he can't foresee the best course of action for himself and his mom.

Of course anxiety can be triggered by feeling overwhelmed in the moment, but even those feelings are grounded in fear about the future. "How will I get all of this done?" "If the kids don't stop yelling, I'm going to tear my hair out." "This damned traffic is going to make me late again." As author and thought leader Eckhart Tolle says, "Unease, anxiety, tension, stress, worry—all forms of fear—are cause by too much future, and not enough presence." It is our projected thoughts about a situation, not the situation itself, that causes us pain. To manage stress and anxiety, you must return to present moment again and again and again. It is in the present moment that you find peace, and it is there you discover the beauty and perfection of life, even in the most difficult circumstances.

The Illusion of Future Perfection

We have trained ourselves to believe that once we calibrate everything perfectly on the outside of our lives, we'll find the peace and perfection we long for. Once our husband lands the perfect job. Once we get the new iPhone. Once we find the perfect lover. Once we lose thirty pounds. Once we earn $100,000 a year. Once our kids make the honor roll. Then we can be happy. But here is the big "aha" . . .

There is no "can be happy." There is only happy now. There is only this moment, and you are happy in it because it is perfect. You have everything you need right now.

Maybe you read the previous sentence several times, and for a second you absolutely grasped the truth of it. But then like a dream, it slips away. How can you be happy now when there's so much to worry about? How can you be happy, even when you really want to, when you feel so damned tired, overwhelmed, and stressed out? There is only one way, and that is to practice presence in everything you do. You don't need to fix or change anything. Just be present. "You find peace not by rearranging the circumstances of your life," reminds Eckhart Tolle, "but by realizing who you are at the deepest level."

When you find your mind ruminating on the past or future, become the loving parent who gently guides the toddler away from the busy street and back to safe ground. Redirect your thoughts away from worry or regret and return to the moment. When you find your heart racing and anxiety bubbling up in your chest, go back to your breathing with loving compassion for yourself. When you find yourself suffering with longing for something or someone you don't possess, look around you and express gratitude for everything in your vision. "I am grateful for this window, this view, this chair, the air I breathe, this cup of coffee, this warm sweater. I have everything I need right now."

When you find yourself crying, despondent, wounded, and in pain, acknowledge to yourself, "I am crying. I am despondent. I am wounded. I am in pain." Sit with these feelings and don't resist them. Simply feel the feelings and embrace them without judgment, and you will see how they pass in time—just as everything passes in time. Attempt to view everything in your life as the neutral observer, even when emotions are overwhelming. Don't add another layer of suffering by fretting over your suffering.

Imagine this: you are captain of a small boat on the river of life. Your job is simply to stay at the helm and keep the boat moving. All things that happen on the shore are the events of your life. You observe them from the perspective of a passer-by. Sometimes the events of life disrupt your boat and cause ripples or waves, but you keep going because you know smoother waters are ahead. Sometimes the river presents obstacles or directional choices, and when you encounter these, you take the best action you know how to take in the moment. Life unfolds as it will. The only thing you really control is your boat and what is happening now.

Live in the Moment, Plan for the Future

The logical next question is, "What about goals and disaster insurance and planning for the future. It's not realistic to be present all the time if I want a better, safer, more successful future." However, when mindfulness is a way of life, everything you do is a present moment activity—and that includes planning and setting goals. Rather than worrying about the future, you set aside a time to mindfully plan for it. Rather than holding back peace of mind and happiness while you await an outcome, you can enjoy every step along the path. Every revelation, every small insight or action toward your goal or future desire can be savored and celebrated in the moment.

Several years ago, I underwent a profound life transition, as I left a career I'd had for over twenty years in order to find my passion. I was trapped in longing and frustration, not knowing what I was meant to do or how to go about finding out. Although there were many positive circumstances and wonderful people in my life, I couldn't appreciate them because of my agitation and confusion over my career. These feelings tainted everything else. It wasn't until I came to view my passion search as an adventure and focused more on the process than the outcome that I could relax and enjoy life.

As you plan for the future, you may experience tedious, boring, or even painful moments. Rather than resisting or struggling against these, breathe into them, even attempt to embrace them. Become aware of even the smallest value these moments add to your experience of life. Decide the best time to work on future planning, and don't allow the future to intrude on your other present moments. Simply by setting this time aside and handling the future mindfully, you can reduce daily stress, rumination, and anxiety.

Your Mindfulness Practice

As I mentioned in the beginning of this book, you won't be able to maintain present moment awareness 100 percent of the time. In fact, you'll be lucky to achieve it 20 percent of the time, and that's okay. A little mindfulness goes a long way. Although it takes diligence, persistence, and practice to create a habit of mindfulness, once you establish the habit in one area of your life, you'll find you want to implement it in all parts of your life.

I like to play the mental game of imagining I've lost my memory. I've also lost the ability to project into the future. So I'm always in a bubble of right now. I see life as a stack of right nows. Right now I'm typing these words. A few right nows ago, I was eating lunch. It might seem like I'm compartmentalizing my life, but I'm really using mind tricks to focus on the task (or emotion or interaction) at hand.

So how can you apply mindfulness to everything in life?

Here are some thoughts:

In your relationships, you can be mindful by being fully present with the other person. You are fully present by listening attentively, both to their words, expressions, and body language. You are fully present by showing empathy and compassion, by sharing laughter or mutual interest in something, or by offering physical touch. You are fully present by being authentic and kind.

Driving to work, you can be mindful by taking a new route so you're forced to pay attention to driving and the new scenery around you. You can pay careful attention to other drivers by turning off your cell phone and turning down the radio.

Listening to music, you can be mindful by sitting down and closing your eyes as you listen. At least for a few minutes, don't multi-task while listening. Simply be with the music and the feelings the music evokes for you. Hear the instruments and voices singing, and pay attention to lyrics.

Washing your hands, you can be mindful as you notice the way it feels to soap your hands and let the cool water run over them.

Taking a walk, you can be mindful by listening intently to your feet hitting the ground, and the sounds of nature around you. Take in the scenery you observe, the feeling of the warm or cool air, and the smells of being outside.

When you prepare food, you can be mindful as you pay attention to every element of the preparation. Look at each item of food and express gratitude. Chop, stir, mix, and cook with full awareness. Smell the food, identify the colors and textures, and notice your own feelings of hunger and anticipation.

When you eat food, you can be mindful by waiting a moment before you take your first bite. Look at the meal before you and notice how it looks and smells. Express verbal or silent gratitude for all the people involved in the getting the meal to the table. Eat slowly, and savor each bite.

When you are waiting in line or in a waiting room, you can practice mindfulness by noticing each person around you and mentally surrounding them with compassion and loving kindness. See them as a person with feelings and pain, just like you, who deserves your love.

When you are in physical pain, you can be mindful by acknowledging the pain without getting lost in mental loops of fear or judgment. You can visualize embracing the pain with a warm and healing blanket. You can see the pain surrounded by healing light that gets brighter and brighter until the pain is just a small pinprick and then it dissolves completely.

As you go to bed, you can be mindful by noticing the warm and soft feeling of your bed, pillow, and blankets. You can pay attention to your body relaxing and your eyes getting heavy. Notice your rhythmic breathing and the sounds of the house settling or the outside noises. If you have trouble sleeping, rather than getting frustrated, use the time for a meditation or mentally scan your body from toe to head, asking each part of your body to relax.

As you now see, mindfulness can infuse everything you do. When you wake up to the reality and power of now, anxieties dissipate because you are no longer focused on them constantly. You are too busy with experience and awareness. Life is comprised of a series of experiences. You've suffered with a deluge of thoughts about these experiences. Mindfulness invites you to release the thoughts and simply have the experience. No judgments. No second layer of pain, shame, guilt, anger, anxiety, or longing. Only you and your awareness of right now. This practice can be applied to everything you do. The more you apply it, the more natural it will become.

There will be many times when your mind jumps back on the mental gerbil wheel or your emotions spiral out of control. Expect that and be kind to yourself. But with your new awareness, you can return to mindfulness more quickly, knowing it is the antidote to your pain and worry. When you find yourself in this position, go to a quiet place, close the door, acknowledge your emotions, and breathe. It's okay. You are okay.

If you embrace mindfulness as a way of life, you are choosing to reorient your life around the only true reality—the present moment. You're giving yourself permission to release your grasp on the past and the future, in the unconscious hope you can alter or control them. Now you acknowledge the illusory nature of everything except this moment, which is perfect. "Whatever the present moment contains," says Eckhart Tolle, "accept it as if you had chosen it. Always work with it, not against it." In doing so, all of life becomes a gift, and you'll find inner peace and freedom in every step.

Barrie Davenport

Want to Learn More?

If you'd like to learn more about mindfulness, confidence, self-esteem, and other self-improvement topics, please visit my blog Live Bold and Bloom.com for more articles, or check out my online courses, SimpleSelfConfidence.com, PathtoPassioncourse.com, and StickyHabits.com.

Did You Like *Peace of Mindfulness*?

Thank you so much for purchasing *Peace of Mindfulness*. I'm honored by the trust you've placed in me and my work by choosing this book to improve your life. I truly hope you've enjoyed it and found it useful.

I'd like to ask you for a small favor. Would you please take just a minute to leave a review of this book on Amazon? This feedback will help me continue to write the kind of Kindle books that will best serve you. If you really loved the book, please let me know!

Other Books You Might Enjoy from Barrie Davenport

Building Confidence: Get Motivated, Overcome Social Fear, Be Assertive, and Empower Your Life for Success

Confidence Hacks: 99 Small Actions to Massively Boost Your Confidence

Sticky Habits: 6 Simple Steps to Create Good Habits that Stick

The 52-Week Life Passion Project